Hogwarts, Narnia, and Middle Earth:
Places Upon a Time

Also by Rob Smith:

McGowan's Call (Short Stories)
Night Voices (Novel)
Children of Light (Science Fiction)

Rob Smith

Hogwarts, Narnia, and Middle Earth:
Places Upon a Time

Drinian Press/
Huron, Ohio

Visit us online at www.DrinianPress.com.

This book has not been created, approved, or licensed by any person or entity related to the writings or publications of the works of C.S. Lewis, J.K. Rowling, or J.R.R. Tolkien. This work is presented for the purpose of commentary and criticism with an emphasis on educating readers concerning great literary themes.

The Scripture quotations contained herein are from the New Revised Standard Version Bible, copyright © 1989 by the Division of Christian Education of the National Council of the Churches of Christ in the U.S.A., and are used by permission. All rights reserved.

Cover design by Drinian Press.

Library of Congress Control Number: 2007905823

ISBN-10: 0-9785165-6-7
ISBN-13: 978-0-9785165-6-7

DrinianPress.com
Printed in the United States

for

Nancy

Hogwarts, Narnia, and Middle Earth:

Places Upon a Time

Contents:

Introduction

I have been an avid re-reader of the works of C.S. Lewis and J.R.R. Tolkien since the 1960s. More recently, I have followed Harry Potter since his first year at Hogwarts. I am also a novelist, a theologian, and a college instructor in religion and philosophy. It strikes me that Rowling's themes place her in line with the two earlier Oxford scholars. As the characters in her stories have matured over the years, so has my respect for J.K Rowling as an author. Time will tell, but I suspect that the chronicles of the seven years at Hogwarts will stand along with the work of C.S. Lewis and J.R.R. Tolkien whose writing changed the landscape of twentieth century fantasy fiction.

As a writer, I appreciate the way in which Rowling has maintained her characters over the course of their passage from adolescence to adulthood. I realize, from my own work, that the secret behind this is to know the characters from the inside out. The good guys stay good, the bad guys stay bad, and those who are finding their way stray and recover their various paths. Once the characters take hold of the story, the author must allow them to lead the way. As soon as Harry was pronounced "the boy who lived!" the great themes of the novels were unveiled. The themes are wrapped in two words, "How?" and "Why?" How was he able to survive the attack that killed so many, his parents included? And, why should his survival be such a big deal? These are great themes, not only in the world of magic, but in the world of Muggles. Being one myself, I appreciated the window that Rowling opened on a school where these issues were easier to see. From the very first book, it was apparent that Harry Potter was destined to be a great wizard. Yet, his personal question, "Why did I live?" is universal, one that ultimately faces every person on the planet.

There is, however, one thing that has distressed me over the long wait until the final book of the series. I would not have been aware of it were it not for the fact that my wife is the world's greatest Harry Potter fan. She has spent many hours in fan sites and reading books in which every conceivable iteration of character and plot has been proposed and reworked. Whenever a new book in the series was released, the speculations were, for the most part, wrong. Some insisted that Rowling had failed. Others, undaunted, proceeded to apply the same rigorous tools to the next adventure. Over the years, I endured spikes in my blood pressure when prognosticators bragged that *this* and *that* would have to happen because the "patterns" laid out by the author from the very beginning were inviolate.

I must admit that the reasoning sounded a lot like a gambler who had it all figured out with a system that could not, and would not, fail *this time*! It always did! I think that the pundits failed to grasp a few essential truths about the link between the writer and the work. For this I appeal to C.S. Lewis who observed that a story grows out of the mind of an author. In this regard, the writer is a creator of worlds. The story is, therefore, never dependent on a plot design or a formula, but on the will and imagination of its teller. Having said this, a good writer will not resolve a mystery by introducing facts late in the drama. This does not honor the reader. The reader would feel duped, cheated by half-truths as a substitute for the narrator's lack of skill. On the other hand, a story "clicks" when the author meets the reader in the tale, and takes him or her on a journey that uncovers a shared truth.

Now that this tale has ended, I have written my book. It is not about what I think Harry, Hermione, and Ron ought to have done, but about the places J.K. Rowling took me during my reading. I don't know if she actually intended me to go to these places, but it is where I found myself over my years at Hogwarts. It was a good school, one of the better ones that I have attended.

Time

As the title of this book suggests, I am going to freely move between the writings of Rowling, Lewis, and Tolkien. Additionally, I will also incorporate biblical themes. It is not my intention to confuse the readers who are more familiar with one of the works, but not the others. My reason is twofold. First, it might tempt you to read beyond the particular books that have captured your imagination. Second, it's sometimes easier to make a point clear by showing other models or ways to approach the same topic. *Time* is a perfect example. In the twenty-first century it is very easy to keep track of time. We have clocks and calendars almost anywhere you look. There's a clock on the corner of my computer screen and on my cell phone. They shine out at me at night on my bedside table and even flash to tell me when the battery is low or if I need to switch to or from daylight savings.

Despite all this, people in general have not given the subject of *time* much thought. For all that we manage to measure it, time is very poorly understood. Einstein said that time was relative. It slows down as we approach the speed of light. Don't worry; I will not break into a physics lesson. (It isn't my subject area. Not even close!) I do, however, know that the mystery of time is one of the sacred elements of the Bible. (This is my subject area!) The Bible opens with an account of creation that starts out, "In the beginning..." This is the first of two creation stories. The second begins in chapter two with God creating a garden around a newly formed breather. In the popular culture, people believe that the opening chapter of Genesis is about the creation of the universe. Once the reader decides that this is the theme, they are off and running. There are stars and two lights in the sky, plants, animals, and human beings. Everything is called into existence. The meaning of these words has fueled the great debate between those who argue evolution and those who favor creationism. To quote Hagrid, "Codswallop, in my opinion"(Rowling, *Stone* 71).

Science is our invention. The biblical writers didn't care about the subject that we now label *science*. Yes, the

Genesis writer acknowledges One God from whom all things come, but it's not for the purpose of introducing us to a science that parallels what we mean when we talk about the origin of the universe. For the first part, the ancients did not have a vocabulary suited to our way of thinking about science. For example, there was no word in ancient Hebrew that could be translated "universe". The word "earth" did not refer to the planet; it referred to the ground, *terra firma.* In early translations of the Bible the English word "universe" was sometimes used to translate a Hebrew word, but that word would have been more properly translated "eternity."

The writers of the biblical texts were aware that there was a problem with time. The problem is that we live in it and God exists beyond it. In Psalm 90, the poet declares that a thousand years to God is like a "watch in the night" but the lifetime of a human is like grass that wilts in the heat of one day. Time, not science, frames the ultimate question of the meaning of life.

In the Genesis account the first thing created is a "day". This is accomplished when light is separated from dark. Note that this "day" is not caused by the rotation of the planet or sunlight. The sun and moon don't show up in Genesis until Wednesday. Their appearance is given, according to the text, "for signs and for seasons and for days and years." In other words, they are to help us tell time!

The narrative about seven days in the opening chapters of Genesis is about the creation of the Hebrew calendar. A cycle of seven days is created, not to explain astrophysics, but as a tool for humanity. By measuring days, weeks, months, and years, human life on a planet locked in time could be coordinated with the reality of God that exists outside of time. The system is based on the number seven and the number fifty. The seventh day is a day of rest, a Sabbath. The Sabbath begins, according to Genesis at sundown on Friday and ends at sundown on Saturday. It is a most sacred observance. By observing Sabbath, humans share in the rest/satisfaction of God. How holy is it? The Law of Moses does not have a penalty for laziness. (I guess it's assumed that laziness is one of those things that catches up with people anyway!) There were, however, strict penalties for not participating in the observance of the Sabbath. Sabbath is a reminder of sacred time, and here's how it worked to make a year. Six days pass and then there is a Sabbath (7 days).

Seven Sabbaths pass (49 days) and there is a feast day that doesn't count in the next week (the fiftieth day). This pattern happens seven times in a year. Twice a year there are two seven-day festivals that don't count in any regular week. Add them up and you find that the ancient Hebrews followed a solar calendar based on 364 days. Keeping track of all this was the sacred duty of the Priests who counted days by using a particular psalm each day in the worship of the Temple. In other words, human time was to be measured by a calendar aligned with devotion toward God. If you wanted to know where you were in the cycle of the year, you had to stay in tune with the pattern of eternity.

Just as awareness of the structure of time is important to the biblical writers, an understanding of how time functions is important to the stories of Tolkien, Lewis, and Rowling. Each of the three great fantasy writers under discussion sets their stories in time and each gives a different setting. The characters in each of these stories struggle with the meaning of their particular place in time.

In the *Chronicles of Narnia*, C.S. Lewis consciously creates a new time, a new place, and a different science. Throughout the entire sequence of books there is a running puzzle: time in Narnia cannot be calibrated to time in England. A school term passes for the four Pevensies and hundreds of years pass in Narnia. It is in *The Magician's Nephew* (which I still think should be read next to last) that we learn about time in Lewis' created world. He introduced us to the relative nature of time by creating a place, more precisely, a wood that does not exist in any time. He calls it, "The Wood between the Worlds". In this wood nothing ever happens. When the evil witch lands there by accident, she is weak (although she can break off lamp posts bare-handed in London!) Why? For Lewis, like the writer of Genesis, the dilemma for human beings is living in time; being disconnected from eternity. In the battle between good and evil, evil only has power *in time*. Since the Wood between the Worlds is outside all the various *time*s of the worlds in the ponds below, evil forces can hold no power in that place. (I know that I'm probably confusing HP fans who have not visited Narnia. Sorry.) The point is that C.S. Lewis' way to deal with time was to create a new version in another place. That place was also ruled by a different science. Unlike our round earth, Narnia is flat. Again, Lewis is making a point: science and time exist by the will of the Creator. If the Creator wanted a different sort of world, the world would be different. In this way, Lewis is underscoring the non-scientific belief in one God that dominates Judaism. Since God is not a deceiver, any truth that we learn about the nature of the material universe is true. It is not, however, ultimate truth. Ultimate truth exists beyond time. This is one of Lewis' major theological themes. In his theological view, the place beyond time is nothing less than the eternity of God.

J.R.R. Tolkien does not change time, and he does not do surgery on Middle Earth to make it a different sort of place. In one of his letters, the author wrote that the name "Middle Earth" came from the fact that he imagined it as a place like the *middle latitude*s of our own world. *Middle* refers to a place, not to a time between two ages. In fact, he never really tells us much about how the time of Bilbo and Frodo relates to today. He does give us some clues though. One of the most delightful hints is Frodo Baggins' recitation at the *Prancing Pony* in book one of the *Lord of the Rings*. Frodo is put on the spot when guests at the *Pony* ask for a song. The story's narrator introduces the verse by saying, "Only a few words of it are now, as a rule, remembered." He then proceeds to a lengthy comedic poem which, in the second to last stanza, says:

> *With a ping and a pong the fiddle-strings broke!*
> *the cow jumped over the Moon,*
> *And the little dog laughed to see such fun,*
> *and the Saturday dish went off at a run*
> *with the silver Sunday spoon.* (172)

In that moment, the reader recognizes the familiar. Middle Earth is our earth, but not our time. It is an earlier age, a time when immortal elves walked alongside of mortal companions. The trilogy chronicles the end of one age and the beginning of another, the age of humans.

I would be remiss if I did not point out another of Tolkien's "time themes" which provides some insight to the understanding of the Harry Potter series. In *The Silmarillion*, Tolkien gives voice to the mythology that undergirds the meaning of Middle Earth. He compares Elves to Men, the immortal and the mortal. (Actually, elves can be killed so they are not immortal exactly, but they do not die of natural causes.) At the end of the first chapter, Tolkien makes what seems to be a curious observation. The elves who do not die, unless slain or overwhelmed by grief, envy humans who die after a short time. Elves become weary of the world, but have not the gift of death to be their healing. The myth goes on to explain that evil powers have, in time, cast a shadow over death so that men fear it and cannot see that it is a great gift. (Those who have jumped ahead in their minds will see that this is also an understanding that Rowling considers in Harry Potter. There will be more about that later.)

Let me recap before stating the obvious. Lewis creates a different world that can only be reached by magic. Tolkien creates an ancient world that exists as fragments of memory and cannot be reached at all because that age of earth has ended. J.K. Rowling creates a school that you can get to on a steam train! Whoo! Whoo!

Whether you recognize it or not, this is an image of time. Harry Potter takes place in the here and now. It's ironic that so much fuss has been made over the "magic" in Harry Potter while there are so many "un-magical" realities that J.K. Rowling shows us. Okay, getting on to Platform 9 ¾ is a bit of a trick, but, for my money, riding the Hogwart's Express would be worth taking a jack hammer to get through the portal. (No, I am not suggesting anything of the sort being done at King's Cross!)

Harry Potter literally takes place on the door step of our world and in our time. It begins on Privet Drive and gets acted out right under the noses of all us Dursleys on the planet. Don't be insulted that I use "Dursley" as a synonym for non-magical folk. The Dursleys are fairly typical as I see them. They are trying to step up a rung or two on the social ladder and taking inventory on their material wealth. Dudley is learning to do the same. He counts his birthday presents, "Thirty-six… that's two less than last year."(*Stone* 26) They are in denial about things they cannot see, taste, touch or smell. In short, we are they! (Muggles all!)

J.K. Rowling gives us other hints about our Muggle nature. One of the earliest I remember is Hagrid's answer to Harry when he asks in *The Sorcerer's Stone* if they can get all the first year supplies in London. "If yeh know where to go," he answers (84). This is how Rowling is able to hide a world within a world and wrap a different time within our time. Muggles are clueless!

My favorite recitation of this fact is clearly stated by Stan Shunpike, the slightly inept conductor on the Knight Bus in *Harry Potter and the Prisoner of Azkaban*. (If you want to be insulted, consider that Stan Shunpike sees more than we do!) When Harry asks why the Muggles don't hear the bus, he answers:

> Them! Don't listen properly, do they? Don' look properly either. Never notice nuffink, they don'. (36)

In the construction of time, Rowling is telling us that the struggles of the magical world are the struggles of our modern world. The problem for us is that we just don't see correctly.

It's About the Story

There was once a boy, the son of a prince and princess. His parents wanted only the best for him, and they wanted to spare him from the harsh realities of the world. He lived in a fine palace, and when he journeyed out, his parents sent runners ahead to clear the highways of the old, the feeble, and the poor. The boy grew up untouched by the sight of pain, hardship, and suffering.

One day, the servants failed to "clean up" the road and the boy saw something entirely new, a gaunt old man with broken teeth. On another outing, he encountered a diseased person lying by the roadside. During a third trip he saw a dead body. Finally, the boy encountered a holy man and learned from him that there were other paths in the world, paths that would make him renounce the illusion of his protected life and face the truth of poverty, sickness, and death.

The young prince was transformed by these four events that washed away the sheltered perceptions of his otherwise "perfect" life. He gave up his wealth and became a great and wise man. He was, in fact, so great that when he was an old man, he was asked, "Are you a god?"

"No," he answered.

"Then are you an angel or a saint?"

"No. No."

"Then what are you?"

"I am awake."

Of course this is a very old and true story. The young boy was named Siddhartha, but often he is referred to by his family name, Gautama. In his later years, he was called Buddha.

I have given you the skeleton of a story in the hopes that you can see its potential for moving people to awareness. It is about the man who woke up. The magic behind such stories is that hearers also can be awakened by their telling. In a story, the reader shares the selective vision of an author who wants you to see something important. When you actually see, the story clicks. When you are asked later, "What did the story mean?" You might not be able to put forward an answer right away.

This is because there is a difference between what a story does and what it is said to mean. Over-interpretation kills the story. Take this story of Buddha as an example. Some hearing the story for the first time would be moved by it until Siddhartha is identified. All of a sudden, "meaning" kicks in and people of other religious traditions get placed on the offensive. People feel obligated to disavow a story if it comes out of someone else's sacred tradition. It is as if *meaning* always has to trump the power of the hearing. Unfortunately, the sad fact is that it usually does. C.S. Lewis, on the other hand, felt that there was really *only* one story. The myths and legends of ethnic communities over the planet all reflected the one story that could awaken people to life's essential meaning. The awakening of the self to God was most of what mattered.

Lewis and Tolkien discussed this during the gatherings of a group of friends who called themselves the Inklings. They were both enamored by powerful mythological stories. Lewis loved the Old Norse legends. Tolkien was a professor of Anglo-Saxon literature and drew his ideas for rings of power from Beowulf. They challenged each other to write stories that would draw readers into an experience that would be honest and raw. They wished to write meaningful adventures which were not overlaid with anyone else's interpretation. They speculated that people no longer experienced the mystery and wonder of the Bible because they had been told so often what the scriptures said. They carried these explanations into their reading so that it was nearly impossible to hear the stories as fresh literature. Yet, the power is in the story!

Years ago, long before the movie came out, I used to read *The Lion, the Witch, and the Wardrobe* to youth groups at our church. When we'd get to the events at the stone table, where Aslan is taunted, bound, and gagged, even the football players would wipe away tears from their eyes. During Holy Week services, I would read the story of the crucifixion and these same students would be yawning. They already knew this stuff, yada, yada, yada! But it's a similar story, isn't it? This chapter is my disclaimer. I cannot tell you what these stories mean. (Don't let anyone tell you what they mean!) What I share in this book is what these stories made me think about. The story is the thing! For a story to gather readers, it has to be good. These three are!

As a novelist, I know that a story begins with an idea that takes the shape of a picture. C.S. Lewis said much the same thing. In an essay entitled, "It All Began with a Picture," he wrote that *The Lion, the Witch, and the Wardrobe* began with an image of a Faun carrying an umbrella and packages through a snowy forest. He concluded the essay by remarking that even the author would have a difficult time explaining where imaginative ideas come from.

Most stories are this way and anyone who has struggled through a plot will tell you that the characters don't always do what you tell them. This is why I was so distressed when the backseat drivers of the Harry Potter series explained *ad nauseam* how the story had to be written. They had a particular meaning in mind and wanted the interpretation to guide the narrative. In my opinion, following a formula creates only bad stories and a real storyteller has total freedom within imagination. After all, it's about the story!

J.K. Rowling has said that the whole series came to her during a train trip, and I believe her. Some days writing a novel is an absolute chore that takes every effort of will to open the file on the computer and start where I left off. On other days, the story writes itself, and my fingers have to move faster across the keyboard to keep up. Those who believe in formulas will have to keep guessing. Good books don't happen that way.

Another important point is that characters don't exist outside of the story. This may seem obvious, but it is a basic premise that is often violated. Characters are shaped by the mind and values of the author. These are expressed through the story and the events which surround the character. If the hero acts nobly, it is because the story drives him/her through choices that must be made. Take the story of David and Goliath, for example. In a children's story version David becomes the hero, the brave boy who stands up to a bully. Most of us learned the story through that sort of telling, but it is inherently corrupt. While the names of the characters are the same, they have been pulled out of the original story and squeezed into a new one. The biblical account, carefully recorded by the Levitical Priests, is not so lightly told. David's speeches to King Saul and the other troops are not boasting of his bravery, but of the faithfulness of the God of the Covenant. Goliath, according to the story, is not in trouble because David is coming to get him. Goliath is doomed because he has affronted the God of Israel. David's confidence is not in his own might, but in the might of God. In other words, if God wants Goliath dead, a field mouse could do the deed!

What happens to Bible stories is the same thing that happens within "fan fiction." Another author runs off with the characters and places them in a new story. In the new context, the hero is changed. Everything about the hero is derived through the story. Change the story, and the meaning takes on an unintended consequence.

Obviously, I do not like fan fiction. I have read the blogs where a would-be writer claims to write a story that honors the characters and would make the original author proud. To me it's like a stranger picking up my children after school to take them on a pleasant outing to the zoo. While he/she might think it a helpful act, I would consider it kidnapping and call the police. Context matters! If, as a writer, my characters convey my inner thoughts and values then they belong to *my* story and not another's. Recently I heard that some people are going to make Bible action figures. The thought is appalling. People everywhere will be playing the Bible rather than reading it. They will create stories to please themselves and baptize them with biblical names. I expect that, in some cases, the disciples of Jesus will rise up to slaughter those who don't accept their particular formulation of the truth. (Scary, isn't it? It's like Rowling's description of the Ministry of Magic under the leadership of Fudge, Scrimgeour and Umbridge.) With the Bible and all great literature, it is the story and not simply the characters that convey the meaning. Great stories have the power to change readers. When any religion takes the story captive, enforces a single meaning for the words, utilizes enforcement while abandoning an open appeal to the hearts and minds of others, watch out!

Point of View

This book has a subtitle: *Places Upon a Time.* If you haven't guessed it, I think that *time* is a central theme. It is also a part of my point of view as a commentator. The great works that I write about are complete. The original authors have finished their creations, so I have the advantage of seeing all of time spread out before me. Narnia has drawn to an end, the age of Middle Earth has passed, and the gates of Hogwarts under Headmaster Dumbledore are shut. I write with hindsight. (Whether it's 20/20 or not remains to be seen.)

I do, however, have some presuppositions on the subject of how we humans can understand time. This chapter is my way of tipping my hand in advance. Here is my view in a nutshell:

> 1) Humans cannot predict the future in detail;
> 2) Humans cannot always understand the present;

3) Humans can learn by reflecting on past events.

There are several ways in which people gain confidence for the future:

1) Some people try to predict it by unraveling clues;
2) Some people try to affect it by shaping their actions and, finally;
3) Some people believe that the outcome is never really in doubt.

One of the most graphic illustrations of this view is a story from the Book of Exodus. Moses is in the holy tabernacle. He has done all that God has commanded. The narrator in the text says, "The Lord used to speak to Moses like a friend, face to face" (33:11). That being stated, Moses asks God to "show his face," that is, he wants to see a visible manifestation. Instead, this wondrous drama unfolds. God places Moses in a narrow rock cleft. In short, Moses' vision is blocked on the left and the right by walls of rock. (It's like he is wearing blinders.) As God moves across the face of the rock toward the opening, Moses cannot see the approach (it is obscured by the walls of the cleft). When God reaches the opening, God places a hand over it so that Moses cannot directly see. Once God turns, the hand is lifted, and Moses can see. He does not view the face of God, but only the back of God moving away.

The description in this passage is an event where Moses is literally picked up and moved. On the other hand, there are peculiarities about the way ancient Hebrew expressed abstract ideas. It may well be that what is being described here is not an external event, but an internal insight into the nature of God in time. Let me explain.

Hebrew is a picture language. In this way, it is quite different than English. We have a large vocabulary of words that are used to describe feelings and ideas. Abstract words are a product of the Greek culture that shaped western languages. As a result, abstract concepts in the Hebrew Bible are always expressed as images. For example, consider this pair of familiar proverbs. The first is Greek and the second is the Hebrew equivalent:

"In union there is strength." (Greek)

"Two dogs kill the lion." (Hebrew)

We are so familiar with abstract thought that we read the first one as straightforward and literal. It is not. "Union" is not a thing. Okay, a plumber might tell you that a union is a type of pipe fitting, but that's something completely different (as is a labor organization). "Strength" is not an actual thing so much as it is a property of a thing (as in the force of muscle or the tensile strength of metal.) In the Hebrew version, there are no individual abstract ideas, only things. The "things" (dogs and lion) are combined to create a picture which expresses an abstract concept. Abstractions emerge from the picture rather than the words themselves. This distinction in languages exists to this day between the languages of the Orient and the West.

Now, let's get back to the point (sorry about that!) This ancient picture view of time is present in *The Lord of the Rings*, *The Chronicles of Narnia*, and the Harry Potter series. I can't tell you absolutely if this is by conscious design (I suspect it is!) or by unconscious assumption by the author. In any case, each of these major works places its main characters in the same *time dilemma*. They know what has taken place before, they are not sure how things will ultimately end, but they pattern their behavior toward the outcome that they desire. Some of them believe that they have the power to create a future by their own design and some of them want only to see justice and fairness reign in the present moment.

Where a character is positioned on these issues usually determines if they are heroes, antagonists, or the "just confused." The antagonists generally have more confidence in their own potential success than the heroes, who are often plagued with self-doubt.

To understand self-doubt, let's return to the image of Moses in the cleft of the rock. He wants assurances from God. He has requested direct, objective knowledge of God, but is instead offered a glimpse of God's back (in metaphoric terms, "where God has been"). Moses cannot see the direction God will take before it happens. He does not know the mind of God in advance and therefore cannot predict everything that God will choose to do. He also cannot directly see God in the present moment (hand over the rock opening), but when God has passed (through time), Moses can observe where God has been. This sets the stage for a great motif of the Hebrew Scriptures. Confidence in the future is tied to a remembrance of God's mighty acts. Trust for the future is not found in knowing what God will do, but in trusting the nature of God. Nowhere is this more graphically illustrated than in the institution of the Passover feast. At the Seder meal, the deliverance from slavery in ancient Egypt is reenacted in the present tense. (Check it out in Exodus 12:27 and Deuteronomy 16.) No one at a Passover meal can ask, "Did this stuff really happen?" Because the people seated around the table become the living proof of the event. In other words, "if it did not happen, we would not be here remembering a time when God brought *us* out of the land of Egypt." It is a powerful compression of time. The same dynamic takes place in Christian observances, but an emphasis on individual salvation has nearly obscured it today.

Those who cannot trust what happened in the past to give confidence in the future can seek other ways to deal with the uncertainty of the present moment. In ancient Hebrew tradition, future-telling and sorcery were considered an abomination. Though these practices were common among ancient peoples, the Hebrews considered them a lack of trust in God. If you need to know what is going to happen in the future for you to feel safe, you do not trust God. It is as simple as that. Confidence toward the future is grounded on the nature of God rather than the knowledge of what God is going to do before it happens. Indeed, knowing what God will do before it is done places the believer in the very place of God. Though stretched to the limit by prognosticators of all religions, this core concept remains at the center of Judaism, Christianity, and on *the straight path* of Islam. Monotheism maintains that there is only one ultimate force behind creation; God can be trusted; and, the ultimate outcome will express the will of the One.

Having stated this, it can feel very different in the crisis of the moment. The headlines are rife with people whose lives have been marked with tragedy. It is hollow to deny the reality of pain, death, and loss. Pretending that these things do not happen or do not matter in the immediate moment is delusional and cruel. This reality of life in the present moment is a cause for self-doubt, but it does not mean that the self-doubter has lost all confidence in ultimate things.

Magic

The inclusion of biblical motifs as a part of the analysis of the themes of these modern authors is meant to provide an ancient foil on the commentary. These modern sagas are variations on historic themes. It has been well-documented that both Lewis and Tolkien were motivated to create what they considered "modern myths" which would move people to respond differently toward life. Their belief was that myth and metaphor have the power to transform the self. For them, the Bible represented a great transforming power, but it was so over-laden with interpretation that the force of the story itself had been impeded. Lewis, in particular, referred to his Narnian adventures as "pre-baptismal". He hoped that by reading them as fresh stories, his readers would then approach the scriptures differently. It was not that the messages duplicated one another so much as it was cultivating a proper appreciation of *story* as a life-giving force.

Having said this, it would be natural to find biblical themes and values (I will refer to them as motifs) in the works of these two writers. They were good friends in their years at Oxford University, and, with other writers, belonged to an informal group that went by the designation, the Inklings. The origins of this name came from the fact that they were all writers who were moving ideas from the mind to the page. The result of that process was ink on the fingers and an inkling of a thought waiting to be expressed.

J.K. Rowling, as far as I know, does not make a direct claim on biblical themes as did Lewis and Tolkien. She does, however, profess an admiration for the Inklings. She has also endured much criticism from certain segments of the Christian community. In my opinion, undeserved.

At its root, much of the criticism is founded upon a distrust of the concepts of *wizard* and *magic* as being contrary to the Bible. The irony is that many of these same people applaud Lewis' *The Lion, the Witch, and the Wardrobe*, a book that clearly references New Testament theology. Though the world of magic is the setting for Harry Potter, the actual magical context is similar to that used by C.S. Lewis who is venerated as a Christian apologist. (In a classical sense, an "apologist" is one who makes an argument for the reasonability of Christian belief.) Careful examination reveals that in the work of all three writers, the biblical prohibitions against certain uses of sorcery are honored. Here is my overview of the how the biblical motif plays itself out in the works of these three authors:

Magic in the Bible

The Bible itself is against the use of magic. It is prohibited under the Law of Moses and those who practice magic are subject to death (Exodus 22:18, Leviticus 19:26, and so forth). In the Acts of the Apostles (13:10), Luke reports that Paul reprimanded a magician with the words, "You son of the devil, you enemy of all righteousness, full of all deceit and villainy, will you not stop making crooked the straight paths of the Lord?"

On the surface, it seems like modern books in which heroes invoke magical powers would be alien to the Bible. The problem with this (and many topics) has to do with understanding that language and meanings shift over time and across cultures. Why are the biblical accounts so anti-magic when it was viewed as such a powerful force in other ancient societies?

The key is found in the central or core idea of the Scriptures, monotheism. The practice of magic in ancient societies is rooted in polytheism, that is, the belief in more than one god. Polytheism was the cultural standard in the ancient world. As a religious system, it explains why there is *good* and *evil*, why disasters happen, and it opens the way to those who can manipulate the future by paying favor to gods (magical powers) who can shape the future. If a river floods, the god of the river must be angry. If an army is defeated, the protecting god of the conquered must be weaker than the deity of the victor.

In the ancient world, the first act of a merchant traveling to a new city would be to offer sacrifices to the gods of that place. Having appeased the local gods and honoring local customs, business could be conducted. If things in the city went sour, locals could seek out those who offended their gods of protection. (One well-known example of this was Nero's blaming the Christian monotheists for the burning of Rome. It was not that he accused them of setting the fires, but of offending the protective deities of the city by worshipping only one God, a foreign one at that!)

Astrologers, future-tellers, and magicians were considered as spreading distrust in God. If God is all-powerful, why is there any need to know what God is going to do in advance? If there is only one God, and God is the sole creator and sole power within and beyond time and space, can there be any doubt about the outcome of history? Ultimately, the creation can only reflect the will of the creator. There is no other will that has the power to give challenge. In this regard, magicians were people who did not trust the future to God and even believed that a powerful person could bend the unseen forces of the universe to their own design. In short, they sought to place the self (or other forces) as a rival to God. This is the "magic" that is condemned in the Bible. It is the desire to know what God will do before God does it. It is the desire to guarantee a security for the future that is based on advanced knowledge rather than on confidence in God.

The question for this discussion is: "Does the description of *magic* presented by these three authors fit the biblical prohibition?" The answer is both "yes" and "no". As I hope to show, in all three works, the antiheroes seem to be striving after a sense of power that conforms with the prohibited magic. On the other hand, the heroes of all the stories employ a completely different understanding of *magic*. In other words, a critical motif in the three master works is the proper understanding of power. In each case, power is understood in the proper use of what the writer refers to as *magic*.

Narnian Magic

Lewis is the most transparently religious of the three. He and Tolkien even had arguments over the explicit similarities between the Narnia stories and Christianity. He once told a fellow Inkling, George Sayer, that while he didn't want the reader to necessarily notice the Christian parallels, he did want to place these images in their minds so that it could stretch their imaginations. "I am aiming at a sort of pre-baptism of the child's imagination," he said (Sayer 318).

In *The Lion, the Witch, and the Wardrobe*, we see two sorts of magic at work in Narnia, the *magic* of the White Witch and the *Deeper Magic* from before the dawn of time. In the *Magician's Nephew*, these two sorts of magic are sifted. The witch's *magic* is alien to the creation. It was brought into Narnia at the beginning, but only after the creation had begun. Those familiar with the story will recall the scene:

Digory and Polly have used a sort of magic to get into another world. This so called *magic* is actually a technology developed by Digory's Uncle Andrew. It consists of a set of rings that allows them to transport to a wood that seems to quietly exist and grow in the space between times. In that woods are portals to any number of possible worlds, all different.

As an experiment, the two use the new technology to jump into the ancient, nearly extinct world of Charn. In a fit of bad temper, Digory awakens a truly nasty character named Jadis. Through her own cunning, she piggy-backs her way into the wood between the worlds where she becomes weak and fragile. From there, she hitches a ride to London where her vitality and magical powers are alarming. The contrast between her weakness in the timeless wood and her strength in our world is Lewis' way of saying that evil magic only exerts power in time. In other words, it has no place outside of time, and certainly not within the eternity of God.

In an effort to save London from Jadis, the two children use their ring technology to transport the witch out of our world's time and into another. They land in a place that is just beginning its own time. As luck would have it, they also transported a horse, a cabby, Uncle Andrew, and an English lamp post. What they witness is the beginning of a new time. The creation comes through a word, or rather, a wordless song sung by a lion.

I cannot read this part of *The Magician's Nephew* aloud without hearing the Prologue to the Gospel of John:

> In the beginning was the Word, and the Word was with God, and the Word was God. He was in the beginning with God. All things came into being through him, and without him not one thing came into being. (John 1:1-3a)

The Greek text harkens back to the Hebrew which opens the Book of Genesis. The motif that is reinforced is the idea that redemption is build into the fabric of the creation. God did not create a world that unexpectedly turned sour. The New Testament theme maintains the monotheism of Judaism. From the beginning, the will of the Creator contains a sustaining commitment to the creation. In Narnian terms, this is referred to as *deeper magic*. Since it happens prior to the creation of time, the powers that exist only within time cannot know it, nor do they anticipate their own doom. Their power ends at the end of time.

If the truth is told, I would have preferred Lewis to refer to the *deeper magic* as *mystery*. In that way, he would have made a clear distinction between two sorts of magic. Then again, since I am not the author, I will use it to il-lustrate my point. There are two definitions of *magic* at work in the writings of the three authors. One is the illu-sion of power that some utilize to create their own sense of dominance. The other is akin to what has historically been called the *divinium mysterium*, the holy mystery, which reveals a Creator whose will is to bind a people-in-time to the eternal purpose of God. This is not a power that can be wielded. Instead, it is presented as a reality which transforms the believer into a oneness with God.

Magic in Middle Earth

Unlike his friend, Jack Lewis, J.R.R. Tolkien leaves God out of his world of Middle Earth. We know from his conversations with the Inklings, however, that this is not because of a lack of personal belief or commitment. Magic does play a role in the trilogy, but it is almost entirely technological in nature. What appears as magic is often a way to make other things happen. Gandalf's staff, glowing swords, the palantir, knots in ropes that hold fast until they are commanded to release, all these could be replaced by flame throwers, firework launchers, cell phones, night vision goggles, etc. Even the rings of power are inventions that can corrupt the strongest of the mighty. When Frodo offers the One Ring to the Lady Galadriel, she resisted its power, but described how its use would transform her beauty to deep despair.

When Boromir argues that the Ring could be turned against Sauron, and the weapon of the enemy could be used against the enemy, the wise argue that it will not work. Why? Ultimately the technology will reflect the will of its creator. That which was designed for evil purposes will persist in the spread of evil things. If a biblical image of war is plowshares beaten into swords (Joel 3:10), and peace is swords into plowshares (Micah 4:3), then it follows that the technology of war does not fit peace, and the implements of peace do not promulgate conflict. War and peace begin in the mind and heart to shape the implements at hand.

Tolkien wrote in the shadow of the Third Reich. The militarization of the world's powers meant that war was inevitable. It is easy to see how the how the creation of orc fighters and weapons were a parody of then current events. Once the weapon is crafted, its desire is to be used. This is the image of the rings of power. Though they seem magically endowed, they are quite simply the technologies of an enemy seeking power, and not magical at all.

Edith Nesbit (b. 1858) wrote some of the children's books enjoyed by Lewis and Tolkien. "The Aunt and Amabel," for example, describes the adventures of a little girl who travels to *Whereyouwantogoto* via a wardrobe in a guest bedroom. In her story *The Magic City*, she writes, "And there's a dreadful law here- it was made by mistake, but there it is- that if any one asks for machinery they have to have it and keep on using it." Inventiveness is a human trait, not an ethical position. The products of our inventiveness cannot be uninvented. Physicist Freeman Dyson uses the Nesbit quote in the opening chapter of *Disturbing the Universe*. Later in the book he quotes Robert Oppenheimer as a warning against technology. "In some sort of crude sense, which no vulgarity, no humor, no overstatement can quite extinguish, the physicists have known sin; and this is a knowledge which they cannot lose" (52). Of course he was speaking of the development of the atomic bomb. (Ironic that, in our own day, we struggle to keep what we know out of the hands of others. Nuclear proliferation is difficult to stop since everyone knows who wears the rings of power. Some rings cannot be unmade in the cracks of doom, and the tempting words to Frodo ring out in every generation. "Put on the Ring!") Just because science *can* do something, does not mean that the thing *should* be done. In the end, the *undoing* is more difficult than the first. My contention is that there is very little magic in *The Lord of the Rings*, at least not in any super-natural form.

Hogwarts School

The name of the place is: The Hogwarts School of Witchcraft and Wizardry. In spite of this, very little magic, witchcraft, or wizardry seems to take place at Hogwarts (or in the wizarding world, for that matter). By this I am referring to the biblical sense in which the magician is attempting to access some god or demigod to fight against a sacred ground of creation. As with the writings of Tolkien, Rowling makes no mention of God. Hogwarts seems a pretty normal school with uniforms, and academic calendar, final exams, and elective subjects. The main varsity sport (Quidditch) draws the admiration of the student body, and some classes are more interest-ing than others. (Indeed, *Divination* is seen as the most "wooly" and borders on parlor games.)

As in Tolkien, what passes for *magic* is a form of technology that unlocks doors, provides personal transportation, levitates objects, makes useful disguises, and, yes, kills when used in the unforgivable way. In this last sense, the three *unforgivable curses* are so named because they have no use other than to create pain, destroy self-will, and murder. These are not supposed to be taught at Hogwarts, but like every invented technology, uninventing them is the difficult part. How do you remove the known tools of domination and destruction from a new generation?

In one of the most haunting magical events, Voldemort recovers his bodily existence. It is the graveyard scene in *The Goblet of Fire*. You would think that this would be a highly charged moment when Wormtail, the minion of the Dark Lord, would conjure up ancient spirits of power. But, no, there is no conjuring. Peter Pettigrew is stirring a pot and following a recipe. The ingredients are straightforward. Add the DNA of the despised Muggle father to a stewed rudimentary wizard body. That makes the essential body formula. Next, the ego needs to be reconstituted. The "flesh of the servant willingly given" and blood of the enemy taken by force are the final two components. Voldemort is a narcissist. He lives for power while despising his own skin. The illusion of power is only sustained by fearful adoring followers and an enemy to be destroyed. To me this seems less magical than psychological. Voldemort has been faced with his own mortality, but he strives to be immortal. In his new form, he has something to prove to himself and he speaks it aloud: "And I am going to prove my power by killing him, here and now, in front of you all, when there is no Dumbledore to help him, and no mother to die for him" (658).

The proposal is actually quite pathetic. He plans to show his greatness by finishing the business he started years earlier. He is going to show his greatness by killing the fourteen year old that he couldn't kill as a toddler. This is not about magic; it is about delusional thinking that grips those who seek immortality through control of others. As in Tolkien and Lewis, the *magic* in Rowling's books represent a struggle in time. This is vocalized by Professor Snape during an Occlumency lesson. "Time and space matter in magic"(*Prince* 531). Struggles with the Dark Lord are time-limited. By the end of the saga it is quite clear that Rowling shares Lewis' sense of *Deep Magic*.

Dumbledore speaks of it in the first book, *Harry Potter and the Sorcerer's Stone.* The power is love (372).

If the idea that *magic* is simply a form of *technology* seems a stretch, let me offer a bit of evidence in my own defense. In the book *The Abolition of Man*, C.S. Lewis writes a critique of the educational system of his day. (In my opinion, it is still valid!) In this essay, he describes the goal of science and magic as being the same. (Here he is not talking about the scientific quest for knowledge, but uses of science that are aimed at subjugating the world of nature to the control of humans.) I have been using the word *technology* to describe this enterprise. Here's Lewis' analysis:

> There is something which unites magic and applied science while separating both from the 'wisdom' of earlier ages. For the wise men of old the cardinal problem had been how to conform the soul to reality, and the solution had been knowledge, self-discipline, and virtue. For magic and applied science alike the problem is how to subdue reality to the wishes of men: the solution is a technique; and both, in the practice of this technique, are ready to do things hitherto

regarded as disgusting and impious- such as digging up and mutilating the dead (77).

Lewis is careful to point out that he is not talking here about a science that is in the pursuit of knowledge, but those whose discoveries are aimed at the conquest of and exploitation of nature. We employ technology as a means of controlling the natural order of life. It is his contention that such an attitude is destructive to the human race. In the end, people become isolated from the world of nature, and they replace their trust in God with the elevation of their own ego. It is my argument that this sentiment is held in common by all three of the writers under consideration. It is central to all three stories.

Tolkien also equates *magic* with the *machine* (technology) in a letter written in 1950 to publisher Stanley Unwin. He speaks of the characters of a story who wish to make things their own and the morality issues that flow from that plot. These become or lead to a desire for ultimate power which is served by invention. Here are his words:

> ...the sub-creator wishes to be the Lord and God of his private creation. He will re-

bel against the laws of the Creator – especially against morality. Both of these (alone
or together) will lead to the desire for Power,
for making the will more quickly effective, -
and so to the Machine (or Magic). By the
last I intend all use of external plans or de-
vices (apparatus) instead of the inherent inner powers or talents – or even the use of
these talents with the corrupted motive of
dominating: bulldozing the real world, or
coercing other wills. The Machine is our
more obvious modern form though more
closely related to Magic than is usually rec-
ognized. (Tolkien *Letters* 145-46)

J.K. Rowling breathes a hint of the relationship between magic and technology in *Harry Potter and the Half-
Blood Prince.* While a Muggle might consider a flying
broom a real feat of magic, her magical characters think
it well within the range of normal physics. For pure
blood wizard Arthur Weasley, the dearest ambition
would be to fathom a great mystery of the Muggle world.
"To find out how airplanes stay up" (86). In other words,
one person's *technology* is another's *magic.*

Where Loyalty Lies

I hope that you are beginning to see the similar assumptions of each of these three writers. A central element in each is time. Within time, the heroes and antiheroes struggle over the legitimate use of power, and the wild card in all this is *death*. Like it or not, death is a natural reality of life. That being said, the attitude of the characters toward death is a clue to their place in the story. To state it another way, a character's obsession with self-preservation is one of the marks of *evil*.

Having just quoted *The Abolition of Man*, I begin with the fiction of Lewis. Good writers do not *tell* you what the story is about; they lead you into the world of the characters and let you see it with your own eyes. Lewis remains consistent with the theme that evil requires time and that technology is a form of magic that can be ignored in ethical terms. Nowhere is it more clearly shown than in the chapter entitled "The Deplorable Word" in *The Magician's Nephew.*

Queen Jadis has just been awakened from her suspended animation by Digory who is in a fit of selfish, ill-temper. He and Polly find out that she was the cause of the destruction of her own world. While fighting a losing battle against her sister, she unleashed the weapon of ultimate destruction, the *Deplorable Word* (again, magic as a form of weapons technology). In her recitation of the great battles that marked the end of history on Charn, she gives us what amounts to a checklist for evil (paraphrased here):

1. She shows them the hall where many nobles were killed for their rebellious *thoughts.* (People are not held accountable for their actions; they are eliminated for their differences of opinion.)

2. After vaporizing a locked door, she comments: "This is what happens to things, and to people who stand in my way." (People are treated as objects.)

3. Once they are out of the collapsing fortress, she has Digory and Polly survey the landscape of her realm. It is all lifeless dust. She asks, "Does your uncle rule a city as great as this, boy?" (I think she rules a sandbox!)

4. She relishes the memory of when, through the magic of a single word, she destroyed her own world. She goes on to explain, of course, that her use of the Deplorable Word was totally her sister's fault. (Evil tends toward nar-

cissism. It accepts the attributes of power, but never the blame. The victim bears the blame, "Look what you made me do!")

5. When asked about all the innocent people who were killed, she asks, "What people?" When challenged on this point, she states, "Don't you understand?... They were all *my* people. What else were they here for but to do my will?" (Again, narcissism: other people have no right to exist other than to be an extension of the self.)

6. When Digory remarks that in our world the sun is smaller, warmer, and yellower, the witch takes on a hungry, greedy look. "So, yours is a younger world," she says. She shows interest in our younger world because it contains more time, and time is the only possible place for a domain of evil. (40-42)

The pieces are all here. Evil is self-centered, delusional, and time-bound. Values are turned on their heads. People are treated as things, and domination is the ultimate achievement. Behind it all, there is a need to extend time. I think that it is significant that Lewis uses the word dust to describe what was left of the river that had flowed through Charn. It is reminiscent of the second story of creation contained in Genesis 2:4-25. This story is sometimes referred to as the Yahwist account of creation because of the Hebrew name of God that appears there (Yahweh). In contrast to the seven day account of chapter one which begins with water, this Yahwist account is a *dry* creation. It begins with lifeless dust.

In the biblical view, *breath* is a gift from God. It is not just a human thing, but all breathers share it (Genesis 1:30). According to the prehistoric accounts of Genesis' 1-11, it is not until the time of Noah that humans are permitted to take animals as food. Until then, they form a community of creatures which share the breath of God. Even after the provision is made, the taking of an animal's life is subject to kosher slaughter as a reminder of the common gift of breath that is the bond between the human and animal worlds.

In symbolic fashion, the world of Jadis (who is later known as the *White Witch*) ultimately becomes a place of dust. This is in direct contrast to the creation of God, in which the dust is in-breathed to become life. The power of evil is the power to destroy and to reign supremely over dust. The rule of life remains within the creative power of God. This is not a power that can be subjugated except for the illusion that can be created in time. The evil characters in all the stories struggle to make the illusion a reality, and, in each case, their ultimate mission fails.

I remember first reading *The Last Battle*. Like many readers, I was under the spell of Narnia. I wanted this new world of animated trees and talking animals to continue unspoiled. Tirian the King seemed a good sort, maybe a little too laid back in the beginning as if he had been lulled into thinking that evil didn't really exist. When the ape, Shift, begins working his mischief, I found myself urging Tirian into action. Like the Monk in Romeo and Juliet, he seems to always get there too late. Still, as a reader, I knew that everything would have to work out. After all, this was Narnia!

Ape himself was just a materialist. He didn't want to rule the world; he just wanted oranges and bananas. Of course, that was just the beginning and Lewis is telling us that finding personal worth in possessions is an insatiable quest. He wants respect in the form of clothes that make him look human. He wants to be called human. He wants liquor, and, in the end, he wants to run with those who are clever in the use of power, Ginger the cat, Rishda Tarkaan, and ultimately, Tash.

The forces for good are all neutralized. Puzzle the donkey puts aside his better instincts because he has underestimated himself. He thinks that he lacks the cleverness of Shift who outmaneuvers his slow, but accurate reasoning. In short, Puzzle falls for fast-talking.

The pious, like King Tirian and Jewel, are neutralized by their own piety. "Aslan is not a tame lion," is repeated until the words become a hated mantra. Though true, it is a truth cut in half, and a half-truth is the best lie. (Lewis notes this in the chapter about the meeting on Stable Hill: "By mixing a little truth with it they had made their lie far stronger" (723).

What is the other half of the truth? It is the simple statement of Mr. Beaver way back in *The Lion, the Witch, and the Wardrobe*. The Pevensie children had just invaded Narnia through the Wardrobe. At the Beaver's house, Susan asks if Aslan, being a lion, is safe. Mr. Beaver's answer is the truth that is missing from the mantra of *The Last Battle*. "Course he isn't safe. But he's good" (146). Words are not the essential nature of truth. Truth is a quality beneath the words. Essential natures are at work here, good and evil are real, and they are not interchangeable. Lewis is warning that piety by slogan is a weapon of the enemy. Spiritual discernment is another matter altogether.

This last point is significant. The Ape and the forces of destruction begin to say that "Tash is Aslan: Aslan is Tash" (685). For them, neither is anything. Their concern is controlling the present situation, the present moment. As I have been stressing, that is the only place where evil can flex its muscle. Its power is only in time.

Toward the end of the story, the people of Aslan are forced through the stable door. The Calormenes see it as death to their enemies. The beasts and humans who pass through the door find life in a place without time. Looking back through the stable door, they see the world that they have left behind. As the sun goes supernova, they see the "great Time-giant", and the moon comes up in the wrong position. Time and the measures of time are being undone (752-53). Evil cannot exist outside of time.

From that point onward, the new mantra is "further up and further in!" The image here is reminiscent of an earlier work by Lewis, *The Great Divorce.* In this book, the main character is urged to move from the outskirts of heaven toward the center, into the deeper knowledge of God. He is urged to see at last without the restriction of "the lens of Time" (141).

Before breaking off this discourse on Narnia, I will make a comment about the dwarves. At the end of Narnia, they seem to opt out of everything. They insist that they will not be "taken in"(742). The words have a double meaning. When the battle becomes fierce, they avoid confusion by rallying to their own cause. They choose to believe no one, rather than to trust in the wrong one. The results are rather pathetic. Here Lewis is making the case that the decisions that are made in time are eternally significant. In a world of victims and oppressors, there is no ethical middle ground called *observer*. Though they do not fall to the lies of the enemy, neither do they comprehend the pleas of the Narnians. They end up sitting on the edge of a timeless, purified Narnia, while insisting that they are bound in a stinking stable. For Lewis, trying to remain neutral in time while life decisions must be made makes sense only to those who cannot see beyond themselves. Like Rowling's Muggles, the dwarves "Never notice nuffink, they don'." (*Prisoner* 36)

Evil characters like Jadis want the world to be an extension of themselves. The heroes wish only to be a reflection of the reign of The Emperor over the Sea (as embodied in Aslan). In this regard, the role that they play extends even beyond their life in time.

In Lewis' writing, as with Tolkien and Rowling, those who wield power for evil purposes demand absolute loyalty. The White Witch, Sauron, and Voldemort demand groveling loyalty from their minions. This is easily illustrated in the oppressive reign of fear over the native Narnians, the self-mutilating, rat-like devotion of Wormtail, and the total consuming lust that befalls Gollum.

In contrast, the protagonists tolerate independence of thought and celebrate personal triumphs of individuals. For example, at the end of the *Sorcerer's Stone*, it is Neville Longbottom's action that gives Gryffindor the House Cup. At the conclusion of *The Return of the King*, the Lady Galadriel praises Sam for having used her gift well. In *The Lion, the Witch, and the Wardrobe*, the small, silent mice at the Stone Table gain stature and voice (as embodied later in Reepicheep). I choose these *minor* characters to make the point that, in contrast to evil, the characters representing virtue are not driven by ego. Only superficially are these stories driven by the idea of a rise to greatness or fame. Actually, quite the opposite occurs. The *higher* a character rises, the greater their sense of smallness. The real theme of the three collections is the biblical idea of *sanctification*. In the popular opinion of the wizarding world, Harry Potter is famous and great. Harry doesn't feel this way about himself. He sees his dependence on the community which surrounds him, Dumbledore, Hermione, Ron, and even Neville. He does what he needs to do.

Frodo is the hero of all Middle Earth, but he wears no crown, longs for a quiet life in Bag End, and lives with the knowledge that, were it not for Gollum, his quest would have failed completely. Merry and Pippin, the "goof-offs" return to the Shire in the livery of Kings and a hero's welcome (*King* 305).

The Pevensies, Edmund especially, learn the value of loyalty to each other and to a cause greater than themselves. In the end of *The Lion, the Witch, and the Wardrobe* the real power is shown in small hints from Lewis. He simply writes: "How Aslan provided food for them all I don't know…" (193).

From the beginning of the Harry Potter series, Rowling sets her characters on a quest that requires more than individual effort. The very first train ride to Hogwarts chronicled the creation of community. Ron and Harry meet and Hermione soon joins in. As the stakes rise, the community enlarges. The formation of Dumbledore's Army is an example of this. The task at hand requires more than a single brave hero. If Harry's appearance at Hogwarts seems to be the beginning, that is an illusion. The story did not begin with Harry Potter. Flashbacks and visits to the *pensieve* tell us of Tom Riddle, his tragic beginnings, and his own warped choices. But the story did not begin with Tom Riddle. In the *Chamber of Secrets*, Professor Binns (unlike the movie) tells of the rift between the four founders of the school (150-151). In short, the contention between *good* and *evil* (tolerance and intolerance of differences between peoples) is from the beginning. It is Voldemort who keeps insisting that the issue is between himself and Harry, and that this issue is over which great wizard shall dominate all the rest. Those on the side of *the good* recognize that they are one of many players seeking a common noble purpose. Not even Dumbledore, the greatest wizard of all time, tries to lay claim on immortality (or, at least, he has renounced his attempts). His companion, Fawkes, is an ever present reminder of the cycle of life and death. Readers could see this in the very first book when Nicolas Flamel surrenders the Sorcerer's Stone, keeping enough of the Elixir of Life so that he and his wife can set their affairs in order. Dumbledore's assessment is telling:

> "To one as young as you, I'm sure it seems incredible, but to Nicolas and Perenelle, it really is like going to bed after a very, *very* long day. After all, to the well-organized mind, death is but the next great adventure. You know, the Stone was not really such a wonderful thing. As much money and life as you could want! The two things most human beings would choose above all- the trouble is, humans do have a knack of choosing precisely those things that are worst for them." (370)

This passage is a concise summary of Rowling's great theme: the meaning of life is in living, not in fighting to stay alive at the expense of others. Death is a natural occurrence, mistakenly feared, but never avoided. Because of this, the measure of life is not in the ability to stay alive, but in the choice to live well. Using others to hang onto life out of fear of death is like drinking unicorn's blood,

> "… You have slain something pure and de-
> fenseless to save yourself, and you will have
> but a half-life, a cursed life, from the mo-
> ment the blood touches your lips."
> (*Stone* 322)

Living for a larger purpose is the measure of life in time. While there are many examples of this theme, one poignant moment is found in the *Order of the Phoenix*. The Weasleys are beginning to nurse their anger over the fact that they cannot rush to their father who is badly wounded in the Ministry of Magic. Their loss of perspective is redressed in a few words from Sirius Black:

> … This is how it is - this is why you are
> not in the Order - you don't understand
> – there are things worth dying for! (477)

In all three authors there is a clear delineation be-tween good and evil. Evil demands loyalty to the self, and good requires obedience to a cause greater than the self. This larger cause invariably creates a community in which the worth of individuals is respected. In contrast, evil demands minions who suppress freedom of the will. This distinction begs the question of what it means to be human.

True Humanity

The first of the two biblical creation stories tells of the creation of time. The world is laid out in units of days, weeks, months, seasons and years. A culminating moment in this account is the creation of human beings (male and female), and the final act is the creation of Sabbath (Genesis 1:1-2:3). According to the text, the purpose of humanity is to be an "image" placed in the creation. The name of God used in this passage is *Elohim*, an unusual word in that it has a plural ending. This God, though One, speaks in the first person plural as a reigning monarch. "Let us make humankind in our image, according to our likeness" (1:26). This One speaks for all things. As with all ancient Hebrew concepts, it is expressed as a concrete image. Taken literally, humans were made to look like God; they are images or statues placed within the created order.

It is not difficult to understand this dynamic. It is a basic characteristic of human societies. Statues perform a function within cultural systems. The statue or monument erected on the town square becomes a reminder of the one who rules the land. In the United States, we do not have our current politicians on coins or memorialized as in countries with monarchs or dictators. Nevertheless, the patron "saints" of the nation have become the images on our monuments and our money.

How strong is this sense of image? It is deeply rooted in the human psyche. Once a battlefield is secured by an invading army, the next objective is often to tear down the statues. The Genesis narrative is in the form of a kingly command between the Creator and the creation. The role of humanity is literally cast like a statue. Human beings are to be the *image* which represents the reign of God within the creation.

When the Law is given through Moses, a command is given for *imageless* worship (Exodus 20:4-6). *You shall not make for yourself an idol* opens this section of the *Torah*. Modern peoples often simplify the commandment by thinking that it refers to statues. Idolatry is not so simplistic as being a warning against art forms. Personally, I think people gain confidence by dummying-down religious history. "If I have no statues or icons, there can't be idolatry," they think. The commandment, however, was not presented in a vacuum. The writer of Exodus is fully aware of the opening verses of Genesis. An image of the creator has already been placed within the creation. Setting another image in the place of the first is a rejection of the order established by God. This is the core meaning of idolatry. It is a matter of improperly valuing one thing over another; that is, treating something with more importance than it deserves. In this regard, anything that is loved disproportionately is an idol. A book, a cell phone, or a new car can all be religious idols if they stand in the way of being human as God intended. An idol is anything which provides a distraction from the task of being fully alive, fully human in the sense of embodying the creative purpose of God. Students in my introduction classes often say that the Bible is the source of our modern sense of *human rights*. The problem with this is that there are no rights *per se* which are given to humans in the Bible. What humans are given is the capacity for *holiness*. According to these biblical accounts of creation, God's intention for humanity is to image the divine presence. The gift of the *Torah* is the means by which the Covenant people are guided in straight paths. The capacity for holiness is not erased by *the Fall,* and emerges in the New Testament in the teaching of the Apostle Paul.

Here I need to make some comments on the interplay between the first creation story and the second. As mentioned, the first creation story begins with water and culminates with God setting an image within the creation. The second story begins in Genesis 2:4 and is a dry creation. The human is created before anything else (rather than toward the end).

In this account, the world is built around the human who is literally drawn out of the soil. God fashions this being from dust and animates it by breathing life into its nostrils. In this narrative, the world is fashioned around the human. God creates a garden around the human and then proceeds to make animals (fellow breathers). Likewise, the human enters the creative activity by naming the animals. In this account, humans are shown to be the creators of language. In our modern way of thinking, God creates the world and the human creates the way in which we think about the world. At this point it is important to note that language is more than communication. It provides the way in which we structure our thinking. Ideas are converted into words and become part of our conscious thought. The conscious activity of the brain is limited by language and vocabulary. In other words, if you were raised with a different language, you would think differently. (This is one of the problems with understanding peoples from another culture.) The human is placed in the garden with a distinct purpose, namely, "to till it and keep it" (2:15). At this point in the story, the human is not differentiated sexually. In the process of making a companion for the earthling (the literal meaning of *adam*), the woman is drawn out of the human being. When the *adam* sees the woman, he instantly recognizes his kinship, "bone of my bones and flesh of my flesh" (2:23).

The two are the tenants of the garden, charged with the tilling of the soil and the proper use of the creation. In short, they are the gardeners.

The two creation stories exemplify parallel roles for the human family. The opening "wet creation" sets the humans (both male and female) as those who image the reign of God within the created order. The word often

used to describe this biblical motif is *steward*. By defini-
tion, a steward is someone who manages the property of
others. In the first story, humans are gifted with a capacity for holiness, the ability to image the creator. Nowhere
in the Bible is this creative intention revoked. While
some would argue that, for the most part, humans have
not risen to the task, the ideal is never undermined.

In the "dry creation" account, the humans are
stewards of the earth. They are placed in the garden with
freedom and with a warning. Not everything in the creation is intended for human use. They are warned from
eating the fruit of the tree in the middle of the garden.
While this is often characterized as a temptation, the
temptation is the product of the human mind and not
the divine will. For example, when a parent warns a child
not to touch a hot heating register, is the warning a *temptation* or a *rule* that, when broken, will elicit a punishment?
The warning is, in fact, a good thing. It is an honest
statement that has the capacity to prevent pain and injury.
If the child reaches out and gets burned, is the resulting
burn a *punishment* or a *natural consequence*? These are the
issues in the final story of the Garden of Eden. Since the
world does not belong exclusively to the humans, not

everything in it is fit for their use. This is not because God is keeping anything from them (as they suppose), but because they are the stewards of the garden, not the power behind creation. They, like everything else, have a value and purpose that is derived from the One.

As stated, the theme of steward and caretaker persist throughout the Bible. The Hebrew concept of *Torah* reflects the attitude that the purpose of the law is the life and safety of the people of the Covenant, not merely divine rules which require obedience. By living within Covenant, the people draw closer to the holiness which is the function of humanity as the image and steward of the Almighty.

This basic message is underscored for Christians in the New Testament. The Fourth Gospel begins and ends with a literary connection between the Genesis accounts of the role of humanity as steward and caretaker. The writer places the *Word* "in the beginning" and it is not a word at all. It is a life. The concept of the incarnation is the invitation to see in Jesus of Nazareth humanity as it was intended. At the end of the Gospel, the author expands the accounts of the other three Gospels by adding: "Now there was a garden in the place where he was crucified..." (19:41). The Gospel that begins with a Greek paraphrase of the Genesis account, has a garden story of its own. In this garden, Mary Magdalene meets the resurrected Jesus and thinks he is the gardener. Why? Because he looks like the steward of the earth that is meant to define *human*.

The Apostle Paul picks up the same motif in his discussion of the resurrection in I Corinthians 15. In this passage, he refers to the Christ as the *last Adam*, that is, the embodiment of the restored humanity. Becoming human as Christ was human is the great Pauline theme of *sanctification* (the capacity for holiness). With all the talk of being born again, Paul's theme is being transformed into the image of humanity that God set into the creation:

> And all of us, with unveiled faces, seeing the glory of the Lord as though reflected in a mirror, are being transformed into the same image from one degree of glory to another; for this comes from the Lord, the Spirit (II Corinthians 3:18).

For Paul, the goal of the faithful life is to be fully human as Christ was human. (Incidentally, this passage from II Corinthians inspired C.S. Lewis to write what he considered his greatest work of fiction, *Till We Have Faces*.)

Stewardship in Harry Potter

It is easy to see that stewardship or caretaking is a theme in the Harry Potter books. It is a common characteristic of all the members of the forces of good. While it is a task that is laid upon individuals, it becomes a network that unites the central players to a common cause.

In *The Sorcerer's Stone*, for example, Hagrid introduces himself to Harry, and it is a literal description of stewardship. "Rubeus Hagrid, Keeper of Keys and Grounds at Hogwarts" (59). In his own bumbling gigantic way, Hagrid is the protector and guardian of many sacred things. He is the one who bears away *the boy who lived* on the motorcycle of Sirius Black and enters the Forbidden Forest as the caretaker of the misunderstood and maligned. He has little regard for himself, but seemingly inexhaustible empathy for dragons, spiders, three-headed dogs, and hippogriffs. He seeks to find wounded unicorns, and bears the literal pain of being a half-brother to the giant Grawp. He has an unyielding faith that all these creatures can take a rightful place in society. (Though, some will definitely need to be *trained-up* a bit!)

The tasks of nurturing and caring are spread throughout the core of protagonists, and in the series, stewardship is a communal activity. Arthur Weasley, for example, cares for Muggles; and Dumbledore seems to be the conservator of students and knowledge. He appears to be the wizard with true greatness, unmatched in wisdom and skill. He's been offered the post of Minister of Magic, but seems content with the position of Hogwart's Head Master. It is not until the final book, that the reader learns the full story. Dumbledore's wisdom is born of the fact that he has come to know himself. It is not modesty that keeps him from assuming the mantle of Minister of Magic. He shuns that designation out of the self-awareness that he would desire power that could be assumed by the title. To his credit, he resists the temptation.

The temptation for the steward is to forget that the treasures being managed are the property of another. In *The Deathly Hallows*, Rowling reveals great insight into the pitfalls of power and the danger this poses to the steward.

In her wizarding world, the lines between good and evil seem clearly drawn. The Death Eaters are in fearful awe before the power of their Dark Lord. The corresponding source of *good* ought to be the Ministry of Magic. The ministry enforces the rules which protect society and maintain the secret balance between the world of magic and the world of the Muggles. As the stories progress, the reader learns of the Ministry. In *Chamber of Secrets* we find them monitoring magic by under-aged wizards. In *The Prisoner of Azkaban* we learn that they employ Dementors and claim to be the protectors of the world of magic. We also learn that they are not always clear about identifying the real threat. By *The Order of the Phoenix*, their role seems to be controlling the media. You-Know-Who's return would cause panic so they turn on the messengers rather than the threat. The reader is always in a quandary as to whose side is at work in the Ministry. Dolores Umbridge in *The Order of the Phoenix* is the focus of this offense. Eventually the stewardship of Hogwarts is placed in her hands, and the rule of her two-faced morality inadvertently advances the cause of the enemy. While she paints herself as sweet and moral, a horcrux of evil hangs around her neck. In the end, the steward who makes poor choices ends up functioning like an enemy of good.

Stewardship in *The Lord of the Rings*

The role of wizard as steward is also an undercurrent in Tolkien's masterpiece. Two places in particular come to mind. The first is in Book I, *The Fellowship of the Ring*. Gandalf recounts to the Council of Elrond his encounter with Saruman, the chief of the wizarding order. The two had spoken of news carried by Radagast, a wizard friend to the birds and beasts of Middle Earth. But Saruman takes to belittling the community of wizards who serve as the stewards of many things, great and small. He has become more enamored with his own new sense of power:

> "Radagast the Brown!" laughed Saruman, and he no longer concealed his scorn. "Radagast the Bird-tamer! Radagast the Simple! Radagast the Fool! Yet he had just the wit to play the part that I set for him. For you have come, and that was all the purpose of my message. And here you stay, Gandalf the Grey, and rest from journeys. For I am Saruman the

Wise, Saruman Ring-maker, Saruman of Many Colors!" (272)

The steward has forgotten himself and becomes isolated from the community of shared values. When the stewards who rule on behalf of another begin to think themselves the rightful owners, a reign of tyrants begins.

This motif is even stronger in *The Return of the King* when Gandalf addresses the man who bears the title *Steward of Gondor*. In sharply worded conversation, Denethor refers to himself as the ruler of Gondor and this, he claims, is the highest purpose in the world until the king should come again. In this moment, Gandalf defines himself:

> "Unless the kings should come again?" said Gandalf. "Well, my lord Steward, it is your task to keep some kingdom against that event, which few now look to see. In that task you shall have all the aid that you are pleased to ask for. But I will say this: the rule of no realm is mine, neither of Gondor nor any other, great or small. But all worthy things that are in peril as the world now stands, those are my care. And for my part, I shall not wholly fail of my task, though Gondor should perish, if anything passes through this night that can still grow or bear fruit and flower

again in days to come. For I also am a steward. Did you not know?" (31)

Stewardship in Narnia

It is in *The Magician's Nephew* that we see the beginnings of Narnia and the introduction of humans as stewards. Within the story line is the notice that evil was brought into the new world by humans. (Digory and Polly had pulled the wicked Jadis out of England intending to dump her into another world.) The consequence is that the humans shall bear responsibility in this newly created order. Aslan says: "...as Adam's race has done the harm, Adam's race shall help to heal it." (80)

Immediately, Aslan chooses a king, the London cabby. When the cabby protests that he doesn't know much about being a king, Aslan asks: "...can you use a spade and a plough and raise food out of the earth?" (82) This brings us back to the common theme that humans are gardeners who coax life from the soil. Further, Aslan charges him with the rule of the creatures. Imbedded in the responsibility is the image of *king* as *steward*. The kings and queens of Narnia cannot view their subjects as property of the realm:

> Can you rule these creatures kindly and fairly, remembering that they are not slaves like the dumb animals of the world you were born in, but Talking Beasts and free subjects? (82)

(Like Lewis, I have Scottish ancestry. I would be remiss to not advise reading the Declaration of Arbroath. Written in 1320, by this document the peoples of Scotland declared their free allegiance to Robert the Bruce citing also that, were he not to rule fairly on behalf of the people, it would be their right to replace him. The image of king as steward is longstanding as a political ideal.)

Back to Narnia.

Digory is sent on an errand to fetch a silver apple from a distant garden. He is told not to eat the fruit, but to return it to Aslan. When he reaches the garden, he finds that the witch Jadis has already entered and eaten of the tree. She tempts him by declaring that she has tasted immortality in the magical food. If he will not take it for himself, she adds, he would be thoughtless and cruel to not take it for his mother who lies dying in England.

When he returns to Aslan, he faithfully delivers the fruit uneaten. He is given the honor of planting the fruit in the heart of Narnia as a protection against the Witch. Aslan explains why Jadis would now loathe that which was stolen and find no joy in the immortality she had attended to steal. In contrast, Aslan makes a gift of the fruit to Digory. This in turn brings proper healing to his mother who lies a world away and sick in bed.

In *The Lion, the Witch, and the Wardrobe*, Aslan speaks again to the Witch's error:

> It means," said Aslan, "that though the Witch knew the Deep Magic, there is a magic deeper still which she did not know. Her knowledge goes back only to the dawn of time. (184)

The theme which ties humanity to stewardship now touches the motif that evil only exerts power in time. Truths from beyond time, that is, eternal truths are unknowable for who seek to use power to dominate the world of time. For C.S. Lewis, the Deeper Magic is *divine sacrifice*. J.K. Rowling uses the word *love* to describe the redeeming force. In the end, Harry Potter asks Tom Riddle to search within himself for *any* remorse (*Hallows* 741). In this case, Rowling is telling us that regret can be a sign of love left behind. If you want to know what you hold as sacred, you would do well to follow your tears. Often grief and regret are the children of love, and not evil. As Gandalf said to Sam and Frodo at the close of *The Return of the King*: "Go in peace! I will not say: do not weep; for not all tears are evil." (310) All in all, the difference between *love* and *willing self-sacrifice* may be very slight.

The Weapons of the Enemy

I have now returned to my original premise that these great sagas are about time. They represent the struggle between opposing forces for the understanding of time. Evil cannot understand the greater forces that exist beyond time, so it employs an arsenal of weapons with the goal of controlling the present moment. As I write this, I realize how dualistic language becomes. The literary motif of the struggle within time does not require a belief in the battle of cosmic deities. The struggle between the forces of good and evil are encapsulated in time. To those living in time, the struggle seems final, and the opposing forces fairly equally matched. The ancient biblical theme of time stands against this characterization. God dwells in eternity, humans live in time. Time is finite, so the idea of *immortality in time* is absurd. Immortality requires eternity, a territory that cannot be assaulted by armies or evil that is based in time.

This discussion begins to sound like the arguments of Plato and the realm of Ideal Forms. In introduction classes to philosophy, this is when my students say: "thinking like this makes my head hurt!"

Sorry, let me make it as simple as I can.

Think of a *Matryoshka*, a Russian Nesting Doll. They are simply little figures that fit inside a larger figure. Sometimes there are four or five nesting dolls from the largest to the smallest. Imagine a nesting doll with only one inner figure. The inside doll is the world of time. The outside doll, which completely encloses the first, is eternity. Nothing that happens on the inside doll affects the outside doll. If there is a war going on inside the *Matryoshka*, it is invisible from the outside. Those on the inside would think it the ultimate clash between powerful forces. The outside reality is that nothing changes.

This is a silly image that I would not want to push too far, but I use it to illustrate a principle of monotheism. Nothing that happens in time is a threat to God. That God cares about what happens in time is the mystery of divine grace. The biblical message is that there may be a battle waging for the hearts and minds of the human family, but the outcome is not up for grabs between powerful forces. Even the Apocalypse of John, better known as the Book of Revelation is clear to point out that the outcome of a present strife is *not* at stake. What is at stake is the character of the community of believers. Will they be transformed by the violence of the world around them, or will they remain faithful in time? It is not a call to arms, but an appeal to faithfulness. In the end, the transformation of time is an act of God, and the circle of time is closed: "I am the Alpha and the Omega, the first and the last, the beginning and the end." (Revelation 22:13)

I must confess at this point that I subscribe to the traditional interpretation of the final book of the New Testament. The apocalyptic style of the writing was a mask to protect against the scrutiny of the Roman Empire. The Beast whose number is the name of a man (666 or 616 depending on the manuscript) is the Emperor Nero. The book describes, not the end of the world, but the end of an age of persecution. Here, as in the Book of Daniel, the reader is assumed to know the links between the graphic language and the strife of the ancient period. Who could the *Desolating Sacrilege* be except Antiochus IV? (Dan 11:31, Mt 24:25, Mk 13:14) He called himself

Epiphanes ("the manifest God"). Behind his back, he was called Antiochus *Epimanes* ("the insane"). Much damage has been done by teachers who argue from the basis of biblical history, but know so little of it.

When the struggle is viewed from the perspective of dueling forces (usually *us* against *them*), the issue becomes one of power. However, this view of power is an illusion. It's simply the battle for control of the inner doll. The real sense of the whole exists outside the field of battle. My premise is that the motif of time undercuts those who think that these great literary achievements are about *power.* The real theme is moral existence or, to put it another way, to achieve true humanity.

In a reply to a reader, J.R.R. Tolkien wrote:

> Frodo indeed 'failed' as a hero, as conceived by simple minds: he did not endure to the end; he gave in, ratted. I do not say 'simple minds' with contempt: they often see with clarity the simple truth and absolute ideal to which effort must be directed, even if it is unattainable. Their weakness, however, is twofold. They do not perceive the complexity of any given situation in Time, in which an absolute ideal is enmeshed. They tend to forget that strange element in the World that we call Pity or Mercy, which is also an absolute re-

quirement in moral judgement (since it is present in the Divine nature). In its highest exercise it belongs to God. For finite judges of imperfect knowledge it must lead to the use of two different scales of 'morality'. To ourselves we must present the absolute ideal without compromise, for we do not know our own limits of natural strength (+ grace), and if we do not aim at the highest we shall certainly fall short of the utmost that we could achieve. To others, in any case of which we know enough to make a judgement, we must apply a scale tempered by 'mercy': that is, since we can with good will do this without the bias inevitable in judgements of ourselves, we must estimate the limits of another's strength and weigh this against the force of particular circumstances

I do not think that Frodo was a *moral* failure. At the last moment the pressure of the Ring would reach its maximum – impossible, I should have said, for any one to resist, certainly after long possession, months of increasing torment, and when starved and exhausted. Frodo had done what he could and spent himself completely (as an instrument of Providence) and had produced a situation in which the object of his quest could be achieved. His humility (with which he began) and his sufferings were justly rewarded by the highest honor; and his exercise of patience and mercy toward Gollum gained him Mercy: his failure was redressed (*Letters* 326).

It is easy in life and in literature to think that *power* is the primary issue. This is a childish perspective akin to young people who *know* that when they get older they will be able to do *anything they want!* Of course adults know otherwise. Power is the same way. Financial power is attainable. Murder and intimidation (destructive power) are relatively easy. Real power such as sustaining life is not, in the end, a human attribute (though medically, in the short-run, it can often be managed by *magical* machines).

In 1958, Tolkien wrote in another letter to a reader:

> But since I have deliberately written a tale, which is built on or out of certain 'religious' ideas, but is *not* an allegory of them (or anything else), and does not mention them overtly, still less preach them, I will not now depart from that mode, and venture on theological disquisition for which I am not fitted. But I might say that if the tale is 'about' anything (other than itself), it is not as seems widely supposed about 'power'. Power-seeking is only the motive-power that sets events going, and is relatively unimportant, I think. It is mainly concerned with Death, and Immortality; and the 'escapes': serial longevity, and hoarding memory. (*Letters* 283-84)

Hero worship is for people living under an illusion of power. Respect for those who make noble choices is something else entirely. The people who make a difference do not set out to be heroes. They are simply people who, like everyone else, have made choices. Morality requires the identification of the *real* issues and not just exerting power greater than that of the enemy. The key is to retain a sense of humanity in the midst of the struggle. Taking on the weapons and tactics of the enemy may mean that in the process of *victory*, the winners become that which they hate. A poignant literary example of this can be seen in the novel *Dawn* by Elie Wiesel. In that novel, Elisha is a survivor of the Nazi death camps. When he is liberated, he joins the migration of people to Palestine seeking a homeland for the Jewish people. The British are policing the region and have instituted a policy to hang terrorists, in this case, the people fighting for a Jewish state. In retaliation, a British officer, Captain John Dawson, is kidnapped. In the end, Elisha is given the task of the executor.

The British were a part of the forces which liberated the death camps. Now they have become the enemy. Elisha goes to talk with John Dawson. He wants to hate him. He wants to hate him enough to make the execution easy, but it does not work. The soldier is affable, a father with an easy smile and a request that a letter be mailed. At dawn, Elisha carries out his duty. By shooting John Dawson, he has become the Nazi and made his own humanity the victim.

There is a fine line between fighting for a noble cause and hatred. When both sides only hate, the enemy has won the larger battle. J.K. Rowling defines the line in *The Order of the Phoenix*. A battle has been waged in the Ministry of Magic and Bellatrix Lestrange has killed Sirius Black, Harry's Godfather. A powerful sensation of hatred rose in Harry and he cast one of the Unforgivable Curses at Lestrange. The Cruciatus Curse knocked her off her feet, but she recovered quickly.

> Never used an Unforgivable Curse before, have you, boy?" she yelled. She had abandoned her baby voice now. "You need to mean them, Potter! You need to really want to cause pain – to enjoy it – righteous anger won't hurt me for long – I'll show you how it is done, shall I? I'll give you a lesson- (810)

Righteous anger is differentiated from *hatred*. The curses which alienate in the wizarding world are based in hatred. It is no wonder that they are not taught in Hogwarts. Hatred has at its base the view that the other person is less than a person. Where hatred reigns, killing is like *taking out the trash*. The victims may lose their lives, but the perpetrators surrender their humanity. Both Rowling and Tolkien make a point of showing how proximity to the powerful weapons of the enemy wears away the protagonists. The Ring of power becomes an unbearable burden for Frodo, Sam, and even Gollum in *The Lord of the Rings*, and the locket horcrux creates divisions between Harry, Ron, and Hermione in *The Deathly Hallows*. The Resurrection Stone which had been transformed into another horcrux had, in fact, led to the death of Dumbledore who could not resist its power (in *Half-Blood Prince*).

This is why the weapons of the enemy are shunned in all three literary works: The Unforgivable Curses are not taught at Hogwarts. Black sorcery is answered with a clash of steel when Nikabrik tries to bring back the White Witch in the days of Caspian (Lewis, *Narnia* 395). And finally, Boromir teeters on the edge of madness when he tries to force the ring of the enemy from Frodo (Tolkien, *Fellowship* 414).

If hatred is the power wielded by evil, it is therefore a force that only exists in time. But there is another aspect to the *weapons of the enemy*, a pattern that is unknown to those whose knowledge is confined to time. It has already been alluded to in a Tolkien quote where he describes Frodo as "an instrument of Providence" (*Letters* 326). In each of these tales, mercy is a powerful strength (though viewed as weakness by the forces of evil). Mercy (pity) spares Gollum who becomes the final ring bearer. Mercy spares (and changes) Edmund's life in *The Lion, the Witch, and the Wardrobe*. In the Harry Potter series, mercy, pity, compassion and empathy appear over and over again and influence the outcome. Dobby, Kreacher, Draco Malfoy, and even Wormtail are just a few characters who survive out of mercy to play a critical role in the end. The mystery behind this power is that it maintains the humanity of the person and links the world of time to eternity. Mercy and forgiveness make less sense than expediency in a world that is bound in time. However, they make a great deal of sense in a world where choices matter eternally. After all, there are things worth dying for.

If I had to limit myself to one passage in the three bodies of work that illustrates the connection between eternity, values, and our choices in time, it would be a scene from *Further Up and Further In*, the second to last chapter in *The Last Battle*. Emeth, a Calormene "enemy" of Narnia, finds himself in Aslan's Kingdom. He is confused by the fact that he had spent his life in the service of Tash (in the story a demonic power). He meets Aslan face-to-face and asks if he (Aslan) and Tash are one and the same:

> The Lion growled so that the earth shook (but his wrath was not against me) and said, 'It is false. Not because he and I are one, but because we are opposites – I take to me the services which thou hast done to him. For I and he are of such different kinds that no service which is vile can be done to me, and none which is not vile can be done to him. Therefore, if a man swear by Tash and keep his oath for the oath's sake, it is by me that he has truly sworn, though he know it not, and it is I who reward him. And if any man do a cruelty in my name, then, though he says the name Aslan, it is Tash whom he serves and by Tash

his deed is accepted. Dost thou understand, Child?' I said, 'Lord, thou knowest how much I understand.' But I said also (for truth constrained me), 'Yet I have been seeking Tash all my days.' 'Beloved,' said the Glorious One, 'unless thy desire had been for me thou wouldst not have sought so long and so truly. For all find what they truly seek.' (757)

I believe Lewis is making a distinction between words, which belong to the realm of time, and values, which are linked to eternity. True humanity is not based on what is said, but on what is lived.

There is an important biblical motif that addresses the relation between providence and the curses of an enemy. It underlies a belief that evil is ultimately self-destructive. I will briefly cite four common examples from the biblical narrative:

In the opening chapters of Exodus, the Pharaoh fears the threat of a slave uprising. He commands that all the male children born to the Hebrews be thrown into the Nile. One family follows his orders and places their infant son in the river in a floating basket. The result is that the King's order places Moses in a position to become the agent of the Deliverer of Israel. The King's own command sets in motion the events of his downfall.

In the Festival Scroll, *Esther*, the villainous Haman announces the doom that he envisions for Mordecai, but his hateful words become his own sentence of death (Esther 6:4-14). Though God is not mentioned by name in the *Book of Esther*, it is clear that the hand of providence is directed against the enemies of the People of God. Their curses are turned on themselves. The requirement within the people of the Covenant is to stay true to their humanity. Nothing proclaims this virtue more than Mordecai's message to Queen Esther: "Who knows? Perhaps you have come to this royal dignity for just such a time as this" (4:14).

In Matthew's birth narrative (Mt 2:16-24) there is a parallel to the story of Moses' birth. In this case, the King, who should be the protector of the people, commands the death of the male babies in Bethlehem. The family of Joseph escapes to Egypt. Returning after the death of Herod, they find Archelaus in command of Judea and retreat to the Galilee. Like Moses, Jesus is placed in a position to fulfill the requirements of a distinctly Christian method of interpretation, Prophecy-Fulfillment; "He will be called a Nazorean" (2:23).

Finally, with slight variation in the descriptions of motives in the four Gospels, Jesus is delivered to his political opponents who finagle his death. The result is the proclamation of the victory of God over sin and death through his servant, Jesus.

The basic principle in each of these stories is the belief that time is linked to eternity and that what happens in time is eternally significant. This does not mitigate the reality of suffering, and raises a larger issue of justice.

Healing All Hurts

The stewardship model for humanity is an image in time. In the Genesis accounts, it is a role that reflects the relation between the creator and the creation. In this sense, its focus is the world in time.

Biblically based religions have faced the criticism that they are so heaven-oriented that they distract their adherents from the here and now. Consequently, the Judeo-Christian tradition has sometimes been blamed for fostering disregard for the welfare of the planet. Critics are quick to point out that the divine command which is given voice in Genesis 1:28 is an invitation to the despoiling of the planet. "Be fruitful and multiply, and fill the earth and subdue it; and have dominion over the fish of the sea and over the birds of the air and over every living thing that moves upon the earth."

In fact, the Hebrew words used in this verse are particularly strong: *rādā*, "tread" or "trample" (as in a wine press) and *kābaš*, "stamp." Though the humans at this point in the story are vegetarians, they are possessed of great potential power, for good or ill. Humans are quite capable of disturbing the planetary environment. Stewardship as a sacred responsibility means moderating what one has the *power to do* and what one *ought to be doing*. The ethical overtones demand justice for the planet as well as the human community. The strong language underscores the seriousness of the consequences when the stewards begin to think themselves the owners.

The restoration of time is an undercurrent in each of the works. For example, in *The Lion, the Witch, and the Wardrobe*, Lewis describes a Narnia that is trapped in winter. The rule of the Witch distorts the time (in this case, the season). The healing of the troubles is not just related to the arrival of Aslan. Aslan's appearance coincides with the appearance of the rightful stewards. The invasion of Narnia by Peter, Susan, Edmund, and Lucy is a signal of change. (I use the word "invasion" because their last name is Pevensie. Pevensey Bay in Sussex was where William the Conqueror came to shore in 1066 before the Battle of Hastings.)

The link between the reign of Aslan and the arrival of true stewards is made from two rhymes given by the Beavers during the children's first supper in Narnia:

> *Wrong will be right, when Aslan comes in sight*
> *At the sound of his roar, sorrows will be no more,*
> *When he bares his teeth, winter meets its death,*
> *And when he shakes his mane, we shall have spring again.*
>
> (146)

> *When Adam's flesh and Adam's bone*
> *Sits at Cair Paravel in throne*
> *The evil time will be over and done.*
>
> (147)

For Lewis, Narnia represents a sort of goodness in nature that is always under attack by interlopers. The antagonist is either "things that look like humans and aren't" (*Narnia* 146) or corrupt men who harness the animals and cut the living trees. In general, justice is meted out by the appearance of Aslan and the restoration of the natural order, a human steward is set upon the throne of Cair Paravel. This is how healing and justice appears in time. It is always approximate and not final.

Final justice in *The Chronicles of Narnia* takes place in *The Last Battle* when the world comes to an end. As in the Norse legends, Narnia is swept away in the ice of cold darkness. The catastrophe is complete when a giant awakens from his sleep beneath the earth. The giant first appeared in *The Silver Chair* where his name was pronounced, Father Time (646).

Tirian, the last King of Narnia, mourns the loss of his world like the death of his mother (*Battle* 753). But as he explores the new land on the other side of the stable door, he finds that he has lost neither. The close of the seven books in this series provides for a healing that is beyond time and therefore beyond the wearing away that time represents. Lewis, a great animal lover, plays this scene lightly with talking dogs running ahead to sniff out the territory. At one point, a young dog takes exception to the speech of the foreigner Emeth. An older dog tells it to hush adding: "Remember where you are" (757). Ultimately, that's the point, and the prejudicial distinctions fall away. Remember where you are!

Tolkien does not offer such a grand cosmic healing, though he points to a place beyond time. After the destruction of the Ring, Middle Earth is set back to order. It is not achieved quickly or easily.

The process is characterized by Sam Gamgee who uses the gift from Galadriel. The Lady had given him a small wooden box adorned with a rune, a silver "G". She stated that it stood for *Galadriel* and also for *garden* (*Fellowship* 391-2).

In the Shire, as in Narnia, the cutting of the great trees is a sign of the despoiling of the land. When confronted with the destruction, Sam, the gardener, remembered the gift of the Lady. Opening the box, he found soil from the wood of Lórien and a single seed. Frodo suggested scattering the dust in the wind, but Sam reforested the Shire, placing a grain of dust at the base of every sapling. The seed, a single silver nut, was planted in the heart of the Shire, and spring brought a restoration beyond all hopes (*Return* 303).

Other injuries were not so easy to address. Frodo became ill on the anniversary of his wounds. While Sam married and his life seemed to move ahead, the Ringbearer could not recover. On their shared birthday, Frodo is reunited with Bilbo and they pass out of Middle Earth with the Three Keepers, Elrond, Galadriel, and Gandalf. It is the end of the Third Age. Sam is left alone. One of the final entries in Appendix B notes that in the year that his wife Elanor died, "Samwise passed the Towers, and went to the Grey Havens, and passed over the Sea, last of the Ring-bearers" (*Return* 378). The import of these plot elements says to me that Tolkien is telling us that not all ills can be remedied in time.

Rowling's story does not actually end. The world of magic continues. Like Tolkien, she does not provide a cosmic closure. Following the destruction of Voldemort, the delight of victory is tempered by the reality of grief, but healing does take place. In the Epilogue we catch a glimpse of Platform 9 ¾ . There we are told about Teddy Lupin snogging with Victoire Weasley! (*Hallows* 756) This is an image of a world quite different from the one Harry was born into. Harry was the orphan who lived in the cupboard under the stairs. Tom Riddle nurtured his cruelty in a Muggle orphanage. In contrast, Teddy Lupin, another orphan, seems normal, well-liked, and well-adjusted.

The transformation of the Wizarding world can be linked to a choice made by Harry Potter. So much of his life was colored by the choices of others. (Like

Voldemort's decision to go after the son of the Potters rather than the Longbottoms.) Harry's choice came in Chapter Thirty-five where Dumbledore met Harry at King's Cross. His old mentor suggests that Harry might well have a choice of returning to life in the world. The place he was in was described as "warm and light and peaceful" and leaving meant returning to "pain and the fear of more loss" (*Hallows* 722). This was not, however, the choice that he had to make. The real choice was framed by Dumbledore:

> "... By returning, you may ensure that fewer souls are maimed, fewer families are torn apart. If that seems to you a worthy goal, then we say good-bye for the present." (722)

Teddy Lupin seems to me the proof that Harry chose well. He did come back to grief, but he also came back as a nurturing presence to the survivors. To me it seems that Rowling is telling us that there are worse things than dying, but healing takes place in time.

Death and Immortality

Much of the previous chapter is a summary of each author's view of death and immortality. In this chapter I would like to address J.K. Rowling's final chapters because I think she surpasses what Lewis and Tolkien had to say. I don't mean this to belittle or to say that the two Inklings fell short in their goals. Rowling is a contemporary voice, and the world has changed significantly in the half century that has lapsed between these great authors.

Lewis was farsighted, however, and warned us of what was on the horizon. In *The Weight of Glory* he makes a curious remark: "We are far too easily pleased" (26). In the address he was referencing the fact that we run after diversions without understanding what is truly offered in life. My students think that I am anti-technology because I tell them to turn off their cell phones. (I'm not anti-technology; I do my writing on a computer, maintain websites, and I even own a cell phone.) What bothers me is that people no longer seem comfortable with silence and complain about boredom if there is a lapse in the video or soundtrack during their waking hours. Lewis was correct, we *are* too easily pleased. Actually, Dumbledore gave a better warning: "It does not do to dwell on dreams and forget to live..."(Rowling, *Stone* 265).

Rowling is familiar with our modern world and knows that it is not a friendly place for children who are pushed into adult roles before passing through the stages of childhood. She has done something else quite remarkable; she has introduced some to the written word, a format that requires imagination. No offense to movie makers (remember that I am a novelist), but film sticks an image in my brain whereas books make me create them out of imagination.

At the end of *Harry Potter and the Deathly Hallows*, she deals with an issue that the adult world treats with silence. She speaks of death and fear.

The book introduces a new set of icons. On the surface, these seem like the *good* counterparts to the evil horcuxes. Each horcrux carries a piece of the evil soul of Lord Voldemort. He leads the Death Eaters, those who will do anything to hold on to life. The Deathly Hallows seem to be weapons that actually fend off death. There are three: the Elder Wand, the Cloak of Invisibility, and the Resurrection Stone. If the hocruxes are the touchstone for Voldemort's immortality, the Hallows are the Holy Grail for those intent on breaking the power of death. Both are dead ends (pardon the pun).

I teach religion at a state university. Many students think that I am an atheist. This is because I teach at a state-funded university and am obligated to instruct from an academic perspective. (I don't preach for conversion!) Some feel obligated to warn me about the impending doom that awaits me. They even tell me what I must do and say to achieve eternal life. I ask, "If a person is obsessed with saving their own skin, do they really love God or just love what they think God can do for them?"

I come out of a Reformed (Presbyterian) tradition. Liturgically, we use the words "he descended into hell" as a part of the Apostles' Creed. Historically, these words are a late addition to the Creed. John Calvin argued that the fact that they were added late gives credence to their authenticity. (After all, have you ever tried to get something NEW into the church? It does not come easily!) He did not, however, take the phrase to mean that Christ went to some underworld and preached to lost souls. In Reformed tradition, *hell* is separation from God. The phrase *he descended into hell* means that when Jesus confronted his own mortality, he faced fear just as we do. His own death was not an easy thing. As a human being, he faced the crisis of his life alone, but he trusted God. He had placed his life in God's hands, and he placed his death in God's hands. The assertion of the resurrection is the affirmation that God can be trusted. You do not need to know what will come next. You only need to trust the one to whom you go.

I don't want to project my own religious language on J.K. Rowling, but her image of Harry Potter walking into the forest struck a chord. Harry struggles with ambivalent feelings. He had placed his trust in his teacher, Dumbledore. Now his mind is aware that all along, his "protector" was aware that Harry had to die. Dumbledore had taught him that life is defined by our choices, but at this moment, Harry has none. He takes the Snitch from his pocket, Dumbledore's last gift to Harry. It opens, and the final Deathly Hallow is in his hand, the Resurrection Stone. He is no longer alone. Surrounded by those who had gone on to death before him, he is given words of assurance. He lets go of the Stone and is alone again, but the enemy is soon upon him. Empty and unarmed, he meets a flash of green light and the world disappears.

He awakens in an undefined space, but he is not alone. With him is a whimpering pathetic baby who cannot be comforted. Also there is Dumbledore. The place is beyond time, but like the Wood between the Worlds, it doesn't seem to be any specific place. (It's actually, as Harry determines, a junction or embarkation point. It's King's Cross.)

Harry begins to understand what has happened. A part of Voldemort had embedded itself in Harry when his mother had been killed. That shard was the pitiable child. By passing through death, Harry had shed the attachment to his enemy. He now decides to return to life, not because it would be easier or more pleasant, but because there is work to do among the people he loves.

The details contained in the story reminded me of observations and reports made by physicians and psychologists like Elizabeth Kübler-Ross and Raymond Moody. These caregivers documented patients' descriptions of *near death experiences*. The elements in these reports mirror the closing chapters of *Harry Potter and the Deathly Hallows*.

In my own career, I have encountered people in the hospitals with similar stories. Many, like Harry, return to life with a new understanding of what they must do. They also set aside the fear of death.

Theologically, the story underscores a biblical view of judgment. (Here I will probably tread on some toes.) Common characterizations about the judgment of God are plagued with courtroom images of *guilty* or *not guilty*. There are other biblical motifs.

This view is embedded in a story contained in the Fourth Gospel. The disciples of Jesus see a man who was born blind. They ask: "Rabbi, who sinned, this man or his parents, that he was born blind?" (John 9:2)

It is a question about assessing blame. (In the biblical world illness was often viewed as a punishment.) Jesus rejects the question. By his view, the blindness exists so that the power of God could be shown in its removal. In other words, there is a difference between the way divine judgment is affected and the way humans want to assess blame. When this man passed through the judgment of Jesus, the blindness was removed.

For those who don't like theological ideas drawn from narratives, Paul says the same thing directly in his letter to the Corinthians. Paul claims that the work of an individual will be tested (purified) by fire (I Cor 3:10-15). In the end, their life will be preserved, but only that which is their true self. In this regard, the Bible declares that the judgment of God does not destroy, it refines. Having passed through it, you are more yourself than ever.

This is certainly consonant with the scene at King's Cross. Harry Potter and Tom Riddle become distinctly separate. Harry's scar no longer burns, and Voldemort, outside of time, is seen for what he is. Reading this, I was reminded of the dungeon scene in the first book. The parasitic face of Voldemort speaks out of the back of Professor Quirrell's head. "See what I have become?" (Rowling, *Stone* 364)

Imagining the image of the inconsolable child at King's Cross, I'd have to say that the seven intervening years were not good to the one who set his sight on devouring death.

Harry returns. He makes another trip from King's Cross to Hogwarts. This time he is not on a steam train. The battle is all but won. Voldemort struck a blow against his horcrux-self when he blasted Harry. He is on the verge of being an empty shell, beyond remorse, beyond love.

Harry is free to live, and to live without the fear of death. As I have described this phenomenon, it sounds like it may be of interest only to those with a religious perspective. I will now argue that it is not. I admire Rowling's bravery for raising this topic in her literature that many began reading as children only to finish as adults. The series was directed to this climax, from the first book when Dumbledore confesses that the invention of the Sorcerer's Stone "was really not such a wonderful thing" (*Stone* 370), through Nearly

Headless Nick's admission, "I know nothing of the secrets of death, Harry, for I chose my feeble imitation of life instead" (*Phoenix* 861).

Death is one of the dirty little secrets of modern life and technology. Denial, however, does not fend it off, and fear incapacitates. Whether wrapped in religious language or not, it is something that needs to be dealt with in a healthy society. As Erik Erikson wrote more than fifty years ago:

> And it seems possible to further paraphrase the relation of adult integrity and infantile trust by saying that healthy children will not fear life if their elders have integrity enough not to fear death. (269)

Postscript

There are a few final comments that I need to make before closing down this brief discussion of works that will continue to inspire readers and writers. There are many themes in these books and many pieces of story that may have particular meaning to particular commentators. I have tried NOT to get too involved with the details of the stories. This is due to several things. First, it would make a very long book which would stand as a poor substitute for reading the actual writings of three great artists. Second, the story is what really matters. Too much explanation will kill the effect that a powerful story has on a reader. Stories work or they don't. The ones that click have a way of changing readers forever.

Once in an interview I was asked why I write fiction. I said something like, "Because it's the best way I know to tell the truth." A writer has the power to cut out the extraneous and avoid the historians who would argue that it didn't exactly happen in the way it was presented. This may sound strange, but I think that fiction can be a pure form of communication where the ideas of one person meet the imagination of another.

There are also words that I did not use in this commentary, words like *Christ-figure*. This was entirely intentional on my part because such words have come to mean very little. Don't get me wrong, as a literary form it is useful. Billy Budd in Melville's story, for example, was a Christ-figure. Aslan, Gandalf, and Harry Potter all qualify as well because they go to their deaths with resolve of purpose. The reason that I don't use them here is that these words are subject to abuse. Because of their content, people take *Christ-figure* to mean *allegory*. I saw this especially in *The Lion, the Witch, and the Wardrobe*. People have chosen to make Aslan into Jesus and study the lion as if he were the man. The stories are not the same. They are not meant to be pure allegory.

I have had students treat the book as if it were a camouflaged Gospel. They defend this by pointing to a few lines at the end of The *Voyage of the Dawn Treader*.

But there I have another name. You must learn to know me by that name. This was the very reason why you were brought to Narnia, that by knowing me here for a little, you may know me better there. (541)

This is what Lewis calls his "pre-baptismal" intention, not allegory. They are meant to be stories to whet one's appetite for an interest in the scriptures. He does not implore, "If you know me here you know me there." The burden remains that "You must learn of me there!" (The stories are not parallel in major ways. For example, Aslan did not die for all of Narnia, he died only for Edmund.)

Lewis and Tolkien worked, first and foremost, to make stories that would stand on their own merit. They wanted strong stories that challenged readers at the core of their being. I think Rowling fits in that company, too. As written, they stand by themselves, without need for sectarian interpretation. They are useful inquiries into the great search for answers regarding life, death, time and eternity. Regardless of a person's religious beliefs (or non-beliefs), these questions lie directly beneath the surface of being human.

WORKS CITED

Erikson, Erik H.. *Childhood and Society* (second edition). New York: W.W. Norton & Co., 1963.

Dyson, Freeman. *Disturbing the Universe*. New York: Harper & Row, 1979.

Lewis, C.S. *The Abolition of Man*. San Francisco: HarperSan-Francisco, 2001.
_____. *The Chronicles of Narnia*. New York: Harper Collins, 2001.

_____. *The Great Divorce*. New York: Harper Collins, 2001.

_____. "It All Began with a Picture." *On Stories: And Other Essays on Literature*. Ed. Walter Hooper. New York: Harcourt & Brace, 1982.

_____. *The Weight of Glory and Other Addresses*. New York: Harper Collins, 2001.

_____. *Till We Have Faces: A Myth Retold*. New York: Harcourt, Inc, 1984.

Lindskoog, Kathryn. *Journey Into Narnia*. Pasadena, CA: Hope Publishing, 1998. (Included as an appendix is the story "The Aunt and Amabel" by Edith Nesbit.)

Mendelssohn, Isaac. "Magic, Magician." *The Interpreter's Dictionary of the Bible*. Ed. George Buttrick. Nashville: Abingdon Press, 1962.

Moody, Raymond A., Jr. *Life After Life (With a Foreword by Elisabeth Kubler-Ross, M.D)*. New York: Bantam Books, 1975.

Sayer, George. *Jack: A Life of C.S. Lewis*. Wheaton, Illinois: Crossway Books, 1988.

Rowling, J.K. *Harry Potter and the Chamber of Secrets.* New York: Scholastic Press, 1999.

_____. *Harry Potter and the Deathly Hallows.* New York: Arthur A. Levine Books, 2007.

_____. *Harry Potter and the Goblet of Fire.* New York: Scholastic Press, 2000.

_____. *Harry Potter and the Half-Blood Prince.* New York: Arthur A. Levine Books, 2005.

_____. *Harry Potter and the Order of the Phoenix.* New York: Scholastic Press, 2003.

_____. *Harry Potter and the Prisoner of Azkaban.* New York: Scholastic Press, 1999.

_____. *Harry Potter and the Sorcerer's Stone.* New York: Scholastic Press, 1997.

Tolkien, J.R.R. *The Fellowship of the Ring.* Boston: Houghton Mifflin, 1954.

_____. *The Letters of J.R.R. Tolkien.* Ed. Humphrey Carpenter. Boston: Houghton Mifflin, 1981.

_____. *The Return of the King.* Boston: Houghton Mifflin, 1955.

_____. *The Silmarillion.* Boston: Houghton Mifflin, 1977.

_____. *The Two Towers.* Boston: Houghton Mifflin, 1954.

Wiesel, Elie. *Dawn.* Trans. Frances Frenaye. New York: Avon Books, 1970.

 The author:

Rob Smith is an ordained minister who served in congregations for thirty-one years before accepting a position as a full-time instructor in Religion and Philosophy at Wright State University in Dayton, Ohio.

In 2005, he shifted his attention to his own literary efforts by completing several novels and creating a volume of poetry. In 2006, the Frost Foundation of Lawrence, Massachusetts awarded him the Robert Frost Poetry Award and his novel *Night Voices* was published by Drinian Press.

He now resides on Ohio's north coast where he continues to write and works to restore a thirty-year-old British sloop. *Keelhouse*, the sequel to *Night Voices*, is scheduled for release in 2008.

Rob holds a bachelor's degree from Westminster College in Pennsylvania and master and doctoral degrees from Princeton Theological Seminary.

Other books from Drinian Press

Night Voices
by Rob Smith

When an asteroid strike in Antarctica throws the earth into volcanic winter, a small group of sailors seeks refuge away from the forces of destruction. Survival depends on their leaving behind the technologies of the twenty-first century and reconnecting with the rhythms of nature. Surrounded by calamity, these families discover the strength of community that is based on values that extend beyond kinship.

HC: ISBN 978-0-9785165-1-2
PB: ISBN 978-0-9785165-0-5

McGowan's Call
by Rob Smith

McGowan's Call is a collection of short stories and a no-vella that chronicles Davis' path from the river town of Hatteras, Ohio to the suburbs of Dayton. This work of fiction provides a rare insight to pastoral ministry out-side the scandals that regularly make headlines. It is an honest exposé of the real crisis that afflicts those who live in the public eye.

ISBN 978-0-9785165-5-0

Order from your local bookstore or go to
www.DrinianPress.com
for links to online booksellers!

www.ingramcontent.com/pod-product-compliance
Lightning Source LLC
LaVergne TN
LVHW091155080426
835509LV00006B/693